INTRODUCING

The Goat's Cheese

A COOKERY BOOK INSPIRED BY THE GOOD PEOPLE AND GREAT FOOD OF SKERRIES

Please allow us to introduce ourselves.

Fergus, Danny and Pete, three thirtysomethings with a passion for Skerries, Ireland's Tidiest Town! I guess you could say we're from different walks of life, but through our mutual love of the town, the idea of the book was born.

Fergus, born and bred in Skerries, has a history in publishing and has been daring himself to write something for years. Danny, also a native of the town, has a deep passion for food and believes if you can read, you can cook. Pete, a classically-trained chef, moved to Ireland in 2003, setting up home in Skerries.

Out of a shared love of food we came up with the idea for a seasonal cookery book that includes recipes from local restaurants, coffee shops as well as from foodies; a compendium of much that is wonderful about Skerries, including a bit of history, culture and chat, with a particular focus on food.

All of the recipes use locally-sourced ingredients where possible.

We've included some quotes and information about the owners and chefs. Look out for Dougie Stewart's wine tips too. We're proud of this town and so are all of the Skerries people who make up this great community.

We've split the book into four seasons, with food that caters for most tastes. We've also listed, at the beginning, all the businesses and contributors. These good folk are the culinary heartbeat of this wonderful town. We're deeply grateful to everyone who became a part of this aspect of Skerries. Inside you'll find great food and information on events in Skerries throughout the calendar year with details of all the best places to experience the culture of our beautiful town.

All we ask is that you enjoy our book and share it with your friends and family.

We've also left some room for your own special family recipes.

Now go forth, forage and feed . . .

Fergus, Danny and Pete

Contributors
A BIG THANK YOU TO OUR CONTRIBUTORS

The Foodies

Café Jacques	The Windmill Steakhouse	The Watermill Café
Olive	The Red Bank	Aidan's Butcher
Blue Bar	Lef	Brasco's
The White Cottages	Conor McGloughlin Catering	Di Vino
Mick Carroll	D&P Byrne Organic Farm	Ollies Place
Fifty 4	Storm in a Teacup	Bombay House
5 Rock	Stephen Attley	Robert Bullock
Linda O'Rourke	Rockabill	Janet Weldon
Stoop Your Head	Skerries Golf Club	Shoots and Roots
Farm Fresh	The Salty Dog	Liam Dineen
The Brick House	Raff's on the Corner	Hella's Kitchen
LA Bakery	Chopsticks	Terry Roy
Seasons	Des Byrne Butchers	Naomi Beinart
Piccolo	Colin Kelly	David Llewellyn
Egan's Ocean Fresh	Pete Radzwion	Terry McCoy

Words and Pictures

Fergus Gannon	Daniel Geeson	Sharon O'Buachalla
Mark Broderick	Ciara Beggs-Roche	Elaine McDonnell
Declan Langton	Michael Flannery	Agnes Matthews
Hugh Fitzgerald Ryan	Ian Murphy	Shane Hegarty
Anthony Hand		

Technical Assistance

Kevin O'Malley	Jason Kevitt	Lydia Rasztawicka
Tom O'Driscoll	Tristan Fagan	Pat Sheehy
Dave Diebold	Big Dog Digital	Gerry Sheehy

Foreword

By Shane Hegarty

One of the best questions to be asked by a visitor to Skerries is, "Where can I get something to eat?" "Well . . ." you answer, and by the time you're done listing off all the options they could have eaten a three-course meal.

A familiar reaction at the end of their visit is one we've become very used to. "Skerries is such a well-kept secret," they say. "I had no idea there was so much here."
More often than not they are talking about the restaurants and cafés. How they found great food that came with great views, knock-out meals in busy pubs, or surprise dishes in small places, or so many delights in the coffee shops that they couldn't resist going from one to the next to the next again.

Around Ireland, towns have become known as foodie destinations, but Skerries has quietly built its reputation almost through word of mouth and the occasional media discovery. It's been a bit of a secret for so long. That's changing. It's becoming famous for its chicken wings and curries; its prawns and pasta; its cakes and ice-creams.

Since being named Ireland's Tidiest Town, there are more visitors, more mouths to feed, more people to leave with tales of something special happening in Skerries.
In The Goat's Cheese you'll find recipes for every season and for every appetite, served up by the people at the heart of Skerries' thriving culinary culture. Accompanied by brilliant photographs that show off the town, this book is a colourful, fun, and ultimately delicious way of capturing Skerries' food at its absolute best.
We're long past the stage where we have to steal St. Patrick's goat* for a decent meal. There's no better time for Skerries to let the secret out.

*Have you heard the legend of St. Patrick's curse?! See page 25

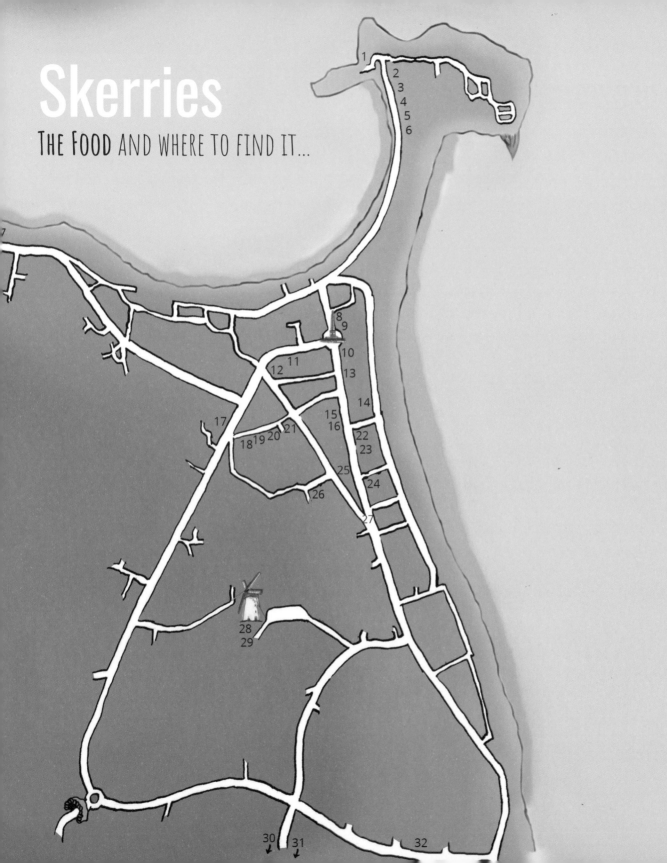

Skerries

The Food and where to find it...

1
2
3
4
5
6

7

8
9
10
11
12
13
14
15
16
17
18 19 20 21
22
23
24
25
26
27
28
29
30 31 32

Photo – Ciara Beggs-Roche

Table of Contents

Summer

Photo - Markbroderickie

Chicken Caesar Salad

Café Jacques, a quaint café situated above Gerry's Supermarket on the main street in Skerries, has one of the most spectacular views in the town. Huge windows overlook the 5 (yes 5!) islands that pepper our coastline. Here's their take on a delicious salad.

Ingredients

2 Chicken Breasts
4 Slices Bacon
40g Freshly Grated Parmesan
2 Heads Baby Gem Lettuce
4 Slices Gluten-Free Bread
Cajun Seasoning
Olive Oil
80g Mayonnaise
1 Anchovy Fillet
1 Freshly-Squeezed Lemon
Salt & Pepper to taste

Method

Caesar Dressing
In a food processor, blend the mayonnaise, grated parmesan (reserve a small amount for plate presentation), anchovy and lemon juice until smooth. Refrigerate.

Caesar Salad
Pre-heat oven to 180°C.
Place bacon in oven and bake for 8-10 minutes.
Slice the uncooked chicken breasts into 12 strips and season with olive oil and cajun seasoning.
To a hot pan, add 2 tbsp olive oil and fry chicken strips for 5-6 mins. Break and wash the baby gem lettuce into a large mixing bowl. Slice your cooked bacon into the bowl and add the cooked/seasoned chicken. Pour in the caesar dressing and mix together. Lightly brush the gluten-free bread with olive oil and toast under the grill.

To Plate
Separate onto two plates and top with the reserved parmesan cheese. Garnish with lightly toasted gluten-free bread.

Gerry's Fresh Foods

Has been located in Skerries for 29 years. Gerry is native to the area, coming from a small farming background. Growing a lot of his own vegetables in polytunnels, Gerry provides in Café Jacques, access to the freshest produce that his loyal customers have grown to love.

RED ISLAND
WINE Co.

Chenin Blanc
South Africa

Harissa Chicken and Quinoa Wrap

OLIVE, ON THE MAIN STREET, OPENED IN 2005 AND HAS GROWN INTO ONE OF THE TOWN'S MOST SUCCESSFUL BUSINESSES. FRIENDLY STAFF, CHARMING ATMOSPHERE AND DELICIOUS FOOD EVERY TIME. EXCELLENT TAKE-AWAY COFFEES AND TREATS TOO. THERE'S SOMETHING FOR EVERYONE.

Ingredients

2 Free Range Chicken Breasts
1 Tbsp Rose Harissa Paste
200g Quinoa
200g Bulgur Wheat
1 Pomegranate
1 Handful Dried Cranberries
1 Handful Pine Nuts
1 Sliced Spring Onion
1 Peeled/Grated Carrot
½ Lemon Juiced
2 Tbsp Extra Virgin Olive Oil
4 Tbsp Natural Yoghurt
1 Handful Chopped Mint
4 Handfuls Baby Spinach Leaves
1 Handful Chopped Parsley
4 Tortilla Wraps
Salt & Pepper to taste

Method

Meat Prep
Pound each chicken breast to an even thickness. Rub the chicken with the rose harissa paste.
Refrigerate for 2 hours (preferably overnight).

Quinoa
In a bowl, add 375ml boiling water to the bulgur wheat and set aside.
Place quinoa into a saucepan with 500ml of water. Bring to a boil and allow to simmer until all the water has been absorbed (5-10 mins).
Mix together by hand the cooked quinoa, bulgur wheat, the seeds of the pomegranate, dried cranberries, pine nuts, grated carrot and spring onion.
Whisk together the olive oil and lemon juice and add to the quinoa mixture. In a bowl, mix the yoghurt and chopped mint and set aside.

Cooking
In a hot pan, fry the chicken breast for approx. 5 mins per side. Alternatively, cook on a BBQ for 10 mins or until cooked throughout.

To Plate
Warm the wraps in the oven for 30 seconds. Spread 1 tbsp of the mint & yoghurt on each wrap. Add a handful of both baby spinach and quinoa salad. Top with half a breast of chicken.
Add some chopped parsley and serve.

Peter and Deirdre Dorrity
Owners of Olive Deli & Café

Peter and I opened our first café, Café Irie, in Temple Bar in 1995 after college and we ran it for ten years before choosing Skerries as a new location to open Olive in 2005. We both completely adore Skerries and it has been the perfect place to raise our three children. It's a privilege to own a business in the heart of such a special, beautiful seaside town and we couldn't do it without the incredible loyalty of our customers at Olive.

Red Island Seafood Platter

Blue Bar - Spectacular sunset views over the only west-facing harbour on the east coast of Ireland. Soak in some summer cocktails and sample the locally-caught fresh seafood. A buzzing family restaurant with great nightlife and live music.

Ingredients

600g Fresh Loughshinny Crab
3 Tbsp Real Mayonnaise
½ Bunch Sliced Spring Onion
1 Beef Tomato (diced)
Salt & Pepper
2 Lemons
60 Dublin Bay Prawns (shelled)
3 Locally Caught Lobster
600g Poached Fresh Salmon
8 Bay Leaves
20 Peppercorns

Marie Rose Sauce (Mix together)
6 Tbsp Real Mayonnaise
2-3 Drops Tabasco Sauce
2 Tbsp Ketchup
5ml Fresh Orange Juice
20ml Brandy
Salt & Pepper

Balsamic Dressing (Blend in hand mixer)
10g Icing Sugar
40ml Balsamic Vinegar
5g Dijon Mustard
10ml Honey
50ml Water
15ml Olive Oil

Side Salad (Mix together)
5 Baby Gem Leaves
60g Mixed Diced Peppers
2 Celery Sticks (chopped)
1 Cucumber (cored and diced)
12 Cherry Tomatoes (sliced in half)
6 ¼-Sliced Lemon Wedges

Method

Seafood Prep

Mix the fresh crab with the mayonnaise, spring onion, diced beef tomato, lemon juice (½ a lemon) and season with salt and pepper.

Boil a large pot of water and a small pot; add 4 bay leaves to the large pot and 1 bay leaf to the small pot. Add 10 peppercorns to the large pot and 5 peppercorns to the small pot. Add a ¼-wedge of lemon to each pot.

Cook the Lobster in the large pot for 9 to 12 mins depending on the size. When they are a smooth red colour place them quickly in a bowl of ice cold water. Remove when cool.

In the small pot, cook the prawns for 2-3 mins and place them quickly in a bowl of ice cold water.

To Poach Salmon

Put the fresh salmon on a 30mm deep tray on greaseproof paper, fill the tray half way with water, add 3 bay leaves, 5 peppercorns and squeeze half a lemon over the salmon. Cover the tray with tin foil. Cook in the oven for 10 minutes at 180°C.

Cool, then refrigerate.

To Plate

Display your selection of seafood and side salad on a white platter with Marie Rose in a small ramekin. Drizzle balsamic dressing on the side salad. Serve with brown bread (see pg 83).

John & Lisa Nealon

Over 25 years living in Skerries, John's family moved here in 1971, buying The Coast Inn. Since then John has opened Blue Bar on the Harbour Road and more recently, 5 Rock close by. Lisa has also opened a shop at the top of the Harbour Road, "The Goat in the Boat". We highly recommend a visit.

PHOTO – DANIEL GEESON

Serves: 4 Cook/Prep Time: 2hrs 20 min

Coronation Chicken Sandwiches

The White Cottages is the number 1 B&B in Skerries on tripadvisor, with a view of the harbour that is second to none. Afternoon tea by the water's edge is a perfect way to relax and enjoy a lazy sunny day in Skerries. Prosecco, if you're feeling adventurous.

Ingredients

1 Whole Chicken (2.25kg)
350g Real Mayonnaise
2 Tbsp White Wine Vinegar
3 Tbsp Mango Chutney
2 Tbsp Salad Cream
4 Tbsp Medium Curry Powder
4 Chopped Scallions
8oz Grapes (sliced in half)
3 Chopped Celery Stalks
1 Tsp Salt
1 Sliced Pan (brown bread)

Method

Roast Chicken
Pre-heat oven to 190°C. Cook for 1 hour 50 minutes for 2.25kg bird. Set aside to cool and refrigerate.

Dressing
In a mixing bowl, combine the mayonnaise, white wine vinegar, chutney, curry powder, salad cream and 1 tsp salt until smooth.

Production
Remove the meat from the whole chicken, discard the skin and dice the chicken into bite-size pieces.
Add dressing to the prepared chicken, enough to cover every piece of meat.
Next add the celery, scallions and grapes and mix well.

To Plate
Use brown bread to make the sandwiches.
Remove crusts and cut into triangles.
Serve with a glass of chilled prosecco and revel at the splendour of the view.

Jackie and Jock

Owners, The White Cottages
Once a petrol station, it is now a guest house and tea venue with a spectacular view. Jackie's parents came to Skerries in the 1960s. Jock is a Skerries native. Together they run a unique and inviting guest house at the top of Hoar Rock.

Seafood Ragú

Local chef **Mick Carroll** knows seafood. He offered us up this delicious seafood Ragú. The rich tomato broth is what makes this dish really special. Try it with tagliatelle if you'd like an italian twist.

Ingredients

8 Dublin Bay Prawns
8 Tiger Prawns
12 Mussels
250g Diced Cod
250g Diced Smoked Coley
(Pollock or Haddock)
4 Scallops (cut into slivers)
1 Carrot (diced-small)
1 Potato (diced-small)
Tomato White Wine Sauce
1 Large Onion (diced-small)
35.5ml Brandy
800g Chopped Tomatoes
½ Tsp Finely Diced Garlic
120ml White Wine
35ml Cream
2 Lemon Wedges
1 Tsp Caster Sugar
1 Pinch Lime Zest
1 Pinch Salt & Pepper
1 Tsp Chopped Fresh Dill

Method

Prep
Steam your carrot and potato for 10 minutes until al dente. Set aside.
Sauce
Cook the diced-onion in a hot pan until soft and translucent. Deglaze with brandy. Add the garlic and chopped tomatoes and cook for 1 minute. Add the wine, dill, sugar, cream and lime zest. Bring to a boil. Reduce to simmer on low heat (approx. 5 minutes).
Production
In a hot medium-sized pot, add 2 tbsp hot water, cover and steam mussels until they open.

Important: discard all mussels that have not opened after this process.

Add the carrots and potatoes.
Add the tomato and white wine sauce and simmer for 3 minutes.
Add the tiger prawns, cook for 30 seconds.
Add the Dublin Bay prawns, cook for 30 seconds.
Add the diced cod and coley and cook for 30 seconds.
Add the slivers of scallop and cook for 10 seconds.

To Plate
Ladle into two large serving bowls and garnish with lemon wedges.

Mick Carroll

It's a lovely little town to grow up in. There's a magic in the people of Skerries and the community comes together when it is needed. It has been a blessing to grow up in such a beautiful town.

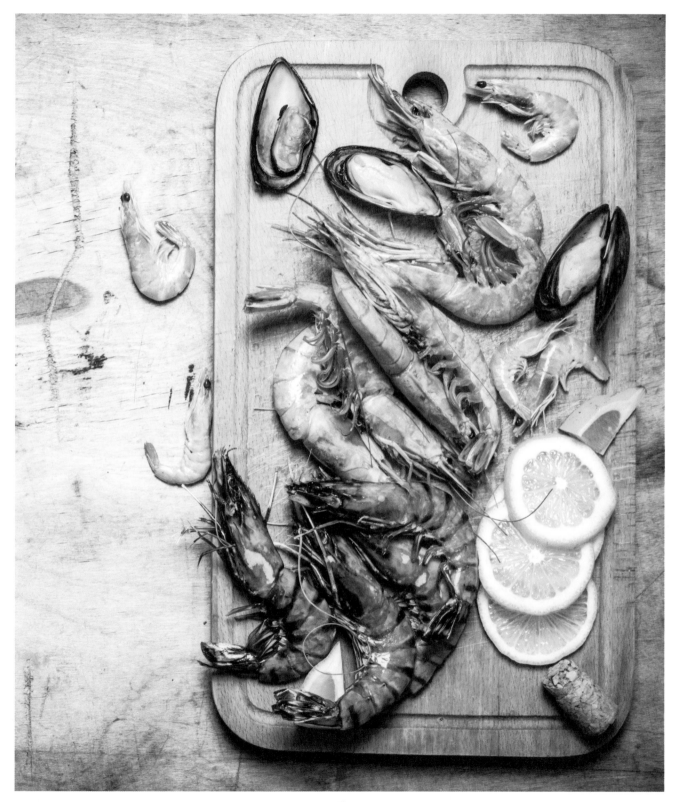

Tequila Chicken with Tagliatelle

FIFTY 4 HAS PERFECTED A CANVAS OF EXCELLENT ITALIAN AND MEDITERRANEAN CUISINE. A WARM, SNUG JEWEL IN THE CENTRE OF THE TOWN. THIS TEQUILA CHICKEN DISH IS ONE OF THEIR MOST POPULAR. WE'RE PRIVILEGED TO SHARE THIS DELICIOUS RECIPE WHICH IS SMOOTH BUT HAS A GREAT LITTLE KICK TO IT.

Ingredients

2-3 Cloves Crushed Garlic
120ml Extra Virgin Olive Oil
115g Chopped Red Onion
115g Diced Mixed Peppers
170g Chopped Jalapeños
2 Chicken Breast (largely-diced)
230ml Cooking Cream
180ml Hot Vegetable Stock
180ml Tequila
Salt and Pepper
170g Grated Parmesan Cheese
Chopped Coriander
Juice of 1 Lime
550g Dried Tagliatelle

Method

Prep

In a hot pan, sauté the chicken in hot olive oil. When nearly cooked, add the onions, garlic & peppers. Cook gently and then tip the pan slightly towards the flame & pour in the tequila (watch out!).
Flambé for a moment before deglazing the pan with the vegetable stock. Reduce by half before adding the cream and Jalapeños. Season with salt & pepper.
Cook the pasta in plenty of salted, boiling water, until al dente.
Combine the cooked pasta with the sauce and add half the parmesan cheese.

To Plate

Serve in warm bowls and top with the chopped coriander, remaining parmesan & freshly squeezed lime (the secret is out!).
Tuck in & Buon Appetito!

John Lawlor

Has been serving up the Italian favourites we've grown to love since Pasta Pizza was established in 1992. John & Tracey often visit Italy for inspiration and motivation.
To all our staff, past & present and to the people of Skerries, we say a big thank you!

Pan Seared & Roasted Lemon Cod

Egan's Ocean Fresh has been providing customers with the freshest of seafood for 4 generations. The fishmongers have been in Skerries for nearly a decade. The guys always have good advice on local seasonal fish and great tips for cooking.

Ingredients

2 x 250g Cod Fillets
(Skin/boneless)
4 Sprigs Fresh Rosemary
12 Vine Cherry Tomatoes
2 Tbsp Olive Oil
2 Tbsp Almonds (Chopped/Sliced)
1 Slice Lemon
Salt & Pepper to taste

Method

Production
Pre-heat oven to 200°C.
In an ovenproof dish, roast the cherry tomatoes on the vine with the rosemary and lemon for 10 minutes.
To a hot pan add the olive oil.
Season the cod with salt and pepper.
Sear for 1-2 mins each side.
On a baking tray place the cod and sprinkle the almonds over the top.
Bake for 3-5 mins depending on the thickness of your fillets.

To Plate
Serve with the roasted tomatoes, garnish with rosemary.
For baby boiled potatoes see pg 89.

Tip: Try soaking the Cod fillets in a shallow bowl of milk for 15 minutes before cooking. This will help take away any fishy odours.

Grilled Beef Skewers

5 ROCK IS A MEXICAN-INSPIRED SMOKEHOUSE GRILL, SITUATED ON SKERRIES HARBOUR WITH AN IMPRESSIVE ARRAY OF COCKTAILS AND CRAFT BEERS. WITH STUNNING WOOD FIRE FEATURES AND A RELAXING AND INVITING INTERIOR, THIS OFFERS A UNIQUE TASTE EXPERIENCE FOR SKERRIES.

Ingredients

450g Beef Tenderloin
1 Red Pepper
1 Yellow Pepper
1 Red Onion
Skewer Sticks (soaked in water)
Chimichurri Sauce
200g Fresh Oregano (chopped)
50g Flat Leaf Parsley (chopped)
1 Red Chilli (deseeded and diced)
25ml Cider Vinegar
250ml Olive Oil
Pinch of Sugar

Method

Chimichurri Sauce
In a food processor, blitz the herbs, chilli & sugar.
While still blending add the vinegar, then the oil until incorporated.
Prep
Cut the beef into cubes, always cutting against the grain.
Set aside a little of the Chimichurri sauce for plating.
Marinate the meat in the sauce for 2 hours in the fridge.
Soak the skewer sticks in water for 5 minutes.
Cut the peppers & onions into large chunky pieces.
Place, in rotation, a piece of onion, pepper, the meat and continue until the skewers are prepared.
Chargrill or BBQ the skewers until medium-rare.

Kate Byrne
Head Chef

I love it, there's nothing else out there for me. I love thinking outside the box, taking chances and trying out new flavours in 5 Rock. I look out the window while at work and the beautiful coloured skies over the harbour every day are a new painting. There's also a great stream of friendly Skerries and visitor faces passing on the street.

Phoenix Pavlova

Linda's Coffee House was the first coffee shop opened in Skerries, so real goats will remember Linda well. We are delighted to be able to include her mouth-watering recipe for this Phoenix Pavlova. Note: Pavlova is not just for russian ballet dancers!

Ingredients

4 Egg Whites
225g Caster Sugar
1 Tsp White Wine Vinegar
1 Tsp Cornflour
1 Tsp Vanilla Extract (essence)
300ml Fresh Cream
Topping: Fruits of your choice

Method

Pavlova Mix
Pre-heat oven to 150°C (140°C fan oven).
Place egg whites in a clean, grease-free mixing bowl. Whisk until they form soft peaks (important: do not over beat egg whites at this stage or the pavlova will collapse).
If using an electric mixer (recommended), reduce the speed and add sugar 1 tbsp at a time, until all the sugar has been incorporated.
Add the vinegar and cornflour (the secret for a soft, marshmallowy centre). This mixture should be stiff and shiny.
Spoon onto a baking tray lined with greaseproof paper.
Bake for 1 hour.

To Plate
Turn off oven, leaving the pavlova inside until completely cooled.
Before filling the pavlova, whip the vanilla extract into the cream until soft peaks form. Invert the pavlova onto a serving plate and fill with the whipped cream. Top with your favourite ripe fruits or berries.

Linda O'Rourke

Skerries is a wonderful place and since coming here as a child on holidays, I always knew this is where I wanted to live. Opening Linda's coffee shop all those years ago was the culmination of a dream I had since I was a teenager. I loved meeting the young and old of Skerries and to this day that's what I miss most about my coffee shop.

Raspberry & Vanilla Bavarois Tart

PICCOLO IS AN INTIMATE CAFÉ-BISTRO WITH HOMEMADE PASTRIES, BREADS AND FRESH PASTA. WELL KNOWN FOR THEIR EXCELLENT ITALIAN COFFEE AND DESSERTS. GEORGIO'S ATTENTION TO DETAIL LEAVES NOTHING TO CHANCE. CHARMING AND HOMELY, WITH EXCELLENT DAILY SPECIALS.

Ingredients

Shortcrust
270g Plain Flour
180g Soft Butter (cubed)
120g Icing Sugar
3 Egg Yolks
3g Salt
Grated Rind of Half Lemon
Grated Rind of Half Orange
375g Fresh Raspberries

Vanilla Cream
3 Leaves Gelatine
100ml Fresh Whole Milk
150ml Fresh Double Cream
½ Vanilla Pod
50g Caster Sugar
3 Egg Yolks

Raspberry Jelly
2 Leaves Gelatine
100g Raspberries
50g Caster Sugar
Garnish
60g White Chocolate (melted)
Drizzle of Fresh Cream

Method

Shortcrust
Preheat oven to 180°C. Quickly knead all the ingredients until crumbly and refrigerate for 1-2 hours. Knead and roll thin (3mm). Place into a pie tin greased with butter, leaving a thin edge crust. Cover the pastry with greaseproof paper (protecting the crust with foil, so not to burn) and fill with dried beans or chickpeas. Bake for 20 mins. Remove and let cool until warm and still soft.
Transfer the tart to a serving dish and brush the base with a thin layer of melted white chocolate (reserve the remaining chocolate for garnish). Cover the pastry with circles of raspberries until filled.

Vanilla Cream
Add the gelatine to a bowl of cool water and soak for 10 minutes. Chill a bowl to use later. In a saucepan, boil the milk with the vanilla pod cut lengthways. In a bowl, whisk together the egg yolks and sugar. Slowly add to the hot milk while stirring vigorously to avoid cooking the egg yolks. Bring the mixture to 82°C, almost to a boil. The cream will be ready when it sticks and coats the back of a spoon. Pass the cream through a sieve and pour into your refrigerated bowl.
Drain the water from the gelatine mix and add to the seived mixture. Stir until the gelatine has disolved. Whip the fresh double cream until soft peaks form. Once the vanilla cream has cooled add the whipped cream. Fold until mixed using a rubber spatula. Pour the mixture over the pie tin filled with raspberries. Refrigerate for at least 2 hours.

Raspberry Jelly
Add the gelatine to a bowl of cool water and soak for 10 minutes. In a food processor, blitz the raspberries with the sugar. Pass the sauce through a sieve to remove the seeds. Heat 2 Tbsp of the sauce, remove the soaked gelatine and mix together until incorporated. Add this mix to the remaining raspberry sauce. Remove the tart from the fridge and evenly spread the raspberry jelly mix. Heat the remaining white chocolate until melted and draw a spiral on the tart, from the centre. Immediately, with a wooden toothpick draw lines from the centre towards the edge; alternate with lines drawn from the edge toward the centre. Refrigerate several hours before serving. Best prepared the day before.

Ingredients

Family Recipe

Title

Method

The Devil to Pay

'Did Brother Fergal ever tell you the one about the saint and the goat?'

It was worth telling again.

The friar nodded.

He had heard it many a time, how the saint took a great lep from his island and how his footprint can be seen in the rock to this day. Didn't he demand his goat back and didn't the people deny that they had it? It was true up to a point, because the goat was eaten.

The butcher from next door, joined them.

'God save you, Friar John,' he said.

He lent his ear to the story.

'The dirty liars', went on the tanner.

'And didn't the goat inside in their bellies hear them and didn't he give a great maa out of him!'

'What was that?' asked the butcher. He loved a yarn.

He was, in his own way, an artist. Whenever he put a carcass to hang on the row of hooks outside his shop, he made little nicks in the outer membrane. As the days went by and the wind and sun did their work, the nicks widened and stretched to form pleasing floral patterns, a florilegium of shoulder, brisket and haunch. He knew by the ripeness of the blossoms when the meat was ready. He also had come for saltpetre to add to his steeping corned beef, the best corned beef in Kilkenny.

He folded his arms as the tanner, out of consideration, began the story again. The tanner fumbled in a satchel and took out a lump of dark bread. He tore a piece off and offered it to the friar.

'No, thank you,' declined the friar, raising his hand. 'Fasting.'

The tanner took no offence.

The ways of the friars were inscrutable. They lived by denying themselves all the simple pleasures of life, God's gifts to men in a hard and cruel world. He spoke with his mouth full. He chuckled at the humour of the story.

'So the good saint put a curse on them. It is a fact that the women of that nation grow beards, like any goat.'

The butcher laughed. 'By the Lord, that would be a sight to see.'

He apologised for the oath.

"That would be a sight.'

With thanks

THE DEVIL TO PAY - HUGH FITZGERALD RYAN

LILLIPUT PRESS 2010 - EBOOK, AMAZON, KINDLE

St. Patrick's Island "Greening"

Photo - Markbroderickie

Autumn

Seafood Chowder

STOOP YOUR HEAD, OR STOOPS TO THE GOATS, IS ONE OF SKERRIES' MOST FAMOUS SEAFOOD RESTAURANTS. ON THE HARBOUR ROAD, BOASTING AN UNFORGETTABLE SEAFOOD CHOWDER, BUT GET DOWN EARLY – IT'S A VERY POPULAR SPOT! ENJOY A PINT IN JOE'S IF YOU HAVE TO WAIT. TRUST US, IT'S WORTH IT.

Ingredients

150g Salmon (skinned & cubed)
150g Cod (skinned & cubed)
150g Smoked Haddock
(skinned & cubed)
450g Mussels in Shells (scrubbed)
1 Finely-Diced Onion
2 Small Diced Celery Stalks
2 Carrots (finely-diced)
60ml White Wine
2 Medium Potatoes
(peeled & diced)
350ml Fresh Milk
200ml Double Cream
25g Butter
25g Plain Flour
200ml Fish Stock
1 Fresh Herb Dill
3 Sprigs Fresh Thyme
1 Juice of Fresh Lemon
Salt & Pepper to Taste

Method

Prep
Melt the butter in a large saucepan, add the onion, celery and carrot and cook for 5 minutes on a low heat.
Stir in the flour to make a roux.
Pour in the fish stock and white wine, add the potatoes and simmer for 10 minutes.
Add the milk and cream. Bring to a boil, stirring continuously.
Add the cubed fish, lemon juice, salt & pepper.
When the fish and potatoes are just cooked add the mussels, dill & thyme. Simmer on a low heat until the mussels have opened.

IMPORTANT: DISCARD ALL MUSSELS THAT HAVE NOT OPENED AFTER THIS PROCESS

Season to taste.

To Plate
Serve in a bowl with brown soda bread (See page 83).

Andy Davis
Executive Chef
Originally from Wales, Andy settled in Skerries because of its location by the sea.
I love Skerries not only because it's a seaside town but also because of its great selection of restaurants and the fantastic local produce.

Tomato and Roast Red Pepper Soup

Farm Fresh offer fresh fruit and veg on sale daily. It is situated beside the stunning new seal sculptures at the carnegie library and floraville. Try this wholesome and nutritious soup to warm you up on a cold autumn evening.

Ingredients

1 Red Pepper
1 Yellow Pepper
(deseeded & roughly-chopped)
1 Small Red Onion
12 Cherry Tomatoes
2 Cloves Garlic (peeled)
1 Tbsp Olive Oil
500ml Veg/Chicken Stock
Sea Salt
Fresh Ground Pepper
1 Pinch Cayenne Pepper
(optional)
40ml Double Cream
(10ml garnish per bowl)

Method

Prep

Pre-heat oven to 180°C.
On a large baking tray, place all of the vegetables, tomatoes and garlic. Drizzle with olive oil and roast for 15 mins.
Remove from oven.
In a large saucepan, add the roasted vegetables, vegetable stock and seasoning (cayenne or to your taste).
Bring to a boil and reduce to simmer for 10 mins.
Remove saucepan from heat and blend with a food processor until smooth. Season with salt and pepper

To Plate

Serve in bowls with a swirl of cream and some fresh brown bread (See page 83).

Catherine O'Brien

Skerries has a uniquely dry climate with a beautiful coastline enjoyed by walkers, locals and tourists.

Quesadillas, Bruschetta & Calamari

THE BRICK HOUSE IS A WONDERFUL, HOMELY RESTAURANT ON THE HARBOUR ROAD, SERVING EXCELLENT TAPAS WITH A FINE A LA CARTE MENU. HERE ARE THREE SIMPLE BUT INCREDIBLE TAPAS THEY SERVE TO ORDER . . . TAMAS AND THE STAFF ARE ALWAYS WELCOMING AND FRIENDLY.

Ingredients

Quesadillas
2 Tortilla Wraps
2 Tbsp Olive Oil
Small Diced Chorizo Sausage
Chopped Spring Onion
Grated Cheddar Cheese
Dried Chilli Flakes
Garnish: Salsa (see pg 118)
Pickled Jalapeños
Caesar Dressing (see pg 3)

Tomato Bruschetta
4 Plum Tomatoes
Handful Finely-Chopped Basil
1 Tsp Dry Oregano
Olive Oil
1 Loaf Ciabatta Bread
Garnish: Basil Pesto (see pg 110)
Grated Grana Padano Cheese

Deep-Fried Calamari
3 Prepared and Sliced Squid
125g Plain Flour
1 Tbsp Lemon Pepper
500ml Sunflower Oil
Sea Salt
Sweet Chilli Sauce (see pg 118)

Method

Prep
To a hot pan add 1 tbsp olive oil.
Reduce to medium heat and add diced chorizo sausage.
Remove and place on paper towel and wipe dry the pan.
Sprinkle cheddar cheese, chilli flakes (optional), spring onion and chorizo on a tortilla.
Top with the other tortilla.
In the same hot pan add 1 tbsp olive oil.
On medium heat, pan-fry the tortilla 2 mins each side or until golden and/or crisp.
To Plate
Cut like a pizza into 4 slices. Plate up and drizzle with Caesar dressing. Garnish each slice with jalapeño and serve with salsa.

Prep
Cut tomatoes into quarters, deseed and roughly-chop.
Mix with finely-chopped basil, drizzle with olive oil and add a pinch of salt and pepper.
Set aside in a small bowl. Pre-heat oven to 190°C.
Slice the ciabatta lengthways, in half. Lightly brush with olive oil, sprinkle with dry oregano and bake for 3-5 mins until toasted.
To Plate
Place the toasted ciabatta in the middle of plate, cover with the tomato bruschetta and sprinkle with fresh grana padano cheese.

Prep
In a shallow frying pan, heat the sunflower oil.
In a mixing bowl add the flour and lemon pepper mix. Add the sliced squid and coat well.
Shallow fry until golden and crisp (3-4 minutes).
To Plate
Remove from oil and place on paper towel. Sprinkle with sea salt. Serve with sweet chilli sauce.

Stuffed Chicken Supreme with Asparagus & Fondant Potatoes

THE WINDMILL STEAKHOUSE IS FAMOUS FOR ITS BEAUTIFULLY-COOKED STEAKS AND WARM INVITING DINING ROOM, BUT IS ALSO KNOWN AND LOVED FOR EXCELLENT SERVICE AND IMPECCABLE FOOD. TRY THIS DELICIOUS CHICKEN SUPREME YOURSELF — AND TRY NOT TO OVER-INDULGE!

Ingredients

2 Chicken Supreme Breasts
(skin on)
100g Goat's Cheese
2 Large Peeled Potatoes
120g Butter
1 Tsp Ginger (finely-diced)
2 Carrots (finely-diced)
350ml Fresh Milk
4 Spears Asparagus
4 Sprigs Thyme
Pinch of Granulated Sugar
Salt & Pepper

Method

Stuffed Chicken Breast
Using a small paring knife, cut into the middle of the large end of the chicken breast. Make a lateral cut within until you have a small pocket and fill with goat's cheese.

Fondant Potatoes
Shape your peeled potatoes into even-sided cylinders.
Place into baking dish lined with greaseproof paper, 60g butter, 2 sprigs of thyme, salt and pepper. Cover with tin foil.
Cook for 40 mins (160°C).

Meat
After 20 mins place the stuffed chicken (skin side down) onto a hot pan. Add 2 sprigs of thyme and cook for 2 mins each side. Place into oven for 20 mins.

Carrot and Ginger Purée
Boil carrots and ginger until just tender.
Drain water, add 60g butter, a pinch of sugar, salt and pepper to taste. Blitz with food processor until smooth.
Boil asparagus for 1 min or until tender.

To Plate
Spread your carrot & ginger purée onto the bottom of a large plate. Slice your roasted chicken and arrange with the fondant potato and asparagus.

Caroline Lacey & Paul Doherty

Are the proprietors of the Windmill Seafood & Steakhouse, located where the original famous Windmill Restaurant used to be on New Street. Both are native to the town, so it has always been a dream of theirs to run a successful and thriving restaurant. No better place than Skerries to make your dreams come true.

Twice-Cooked Succulent Pork

LEF IS AN EXCELLENT CHINESE RESTAURANT WITH A GREAT REPUTATION, DESPITE BEING RELATIVELY NEW TO THE TOWN. OWNER AND HEAD CHEF DAYN SUN HAS CHOSEN A TRADITIONAL EASTERN CHINESE DISH AND GIVEN IT A LOCAL TWIST. THEY DO SMASHING TAKE-AWAYS TOO . . .

Ingredients

1 Pork Tenderloin
½ Egg White
1 Tsp White Wine
1 Tsp Chopped Red Chilli Pepper
½ Tsp Salt
4 Tbsp Cornflour
Small glass of cold water
1 Tbsp Plain Flour
2 Tbsp Granulated Sugar
1 Tbsp Cider Vinegar
2 Tbsp Tomato Ketchup
½ Crushed Chicken Stock
500g Sunflower Oil
4 Finely-Sliced Spring Onions
Chopped Coriander

Method

Pork Marinade

Slice the pork into even strips.

Mix together the egg white, white wine, finely-chopped red chilli pepper and salt. Add the sliced pork.

In a mixing bowl add 3 tbsp cornflour, plain flour and stir in water to make a thick batter. Let stand for 2 mins. Add the sliced pork mixture and coat well. Set aside.

Sweet & Sour Sauce

In a medium saucepan, add sugar, vinegar, ketchup, a pinch of salt, chicken stock, water and 1 tbsp corn flour.

Mix well. Heat to boil and reduce to simmer.

Meat

In a wok, heat 500g sunflower oil to 70°C. Add the sliced pork pieces and fry. Avoid them sticking together.

Cook for 3-4 mins. Remove the pork and rest for 2 mins. Heat oil to 100°C and cook pork for an additional 3-4 mins, until golden brown.

To Plate

Remove the pork and quickly toss into the sweet and sour mixture. Coat well. Serve over your choice of cooked rice. Garnish with spring onion and coriander.

Mackerel

Needs very simple cooking and a really hot grill is best. Fillets are probably easiest to manage and the bone line is easy to spot down the middle. As with all oily fish, mackerel has fantastic nutritional qualities.

Mackerel is a favourite of Skerries, and you'll get them free at the harbour, but bring your rod and feathers!

SKERRIES HARBOUR – 1906

Grilled Mackerel with Devilled Sauce

Conor McGloughlin Catering originated as a retail delicatessen, fish shop and restaurant in 2003 in Rush, county Dublin - the market garden of Ireland. Conor's goal is to prepare delicious food at reasonable prices, served and delivered by friendly knowledgeable staff.

Ingredients

4 Fresh Mackerel Fillets
1 Small Onion (finely-diced)
15 Crushed Peppercorns
3 Tbsp White Wine
3 Tbsp White Wine Vinegar
500ml Veal Stock
(Beef Stock if not available)
Cayenne Pepper
Olive Oil
Salt & Pepper to taste

Method

Devilled Sauce
Put the diced onion in a small saucepan with the white wine, vinegar and crushed peppercorns. Reduce the volume by half.
In a separate pan, reduce the veal (or beef) stock by half, then add both reductions and reduce for approx. 10 mins or until the sauce looks glossy.
Add a pinch of cayenne pepper, then strain the sauce into a clean pan. If the sauce needs thickening, whisk in a little cornflour.

Grilled Mackerel
Season the flesh with salt & pepper. Make 3 cross cuts on the skin side of the mackerel (deep enough to see the flesh under the skin) and place, flesh side down, on a baking sheet brushed with olive oil. Cook under the grill for 4-5 mins or until flesh is cooked through.
For baby boiled potatoes see pg 89.

Conor McGloughlin

Everyone from Skerries has caught a mackerel at some stage in their life, from the end of the pier, off a small boat or just casting a line into the sea. If you haven't yet, you really have to give this a try!
Although a slight exaggeration, it's safe to say that everyone in the town knows someone with a boat.
It is normally around mid-to-late Summer when the shoals of mackerel arrive. You'll notice a few being caught from the harbour and plenty of boats out fishing as well. Freshness is important. Keep your eye out for fresh stiff fish with lovely purple gills. Or ask your fishmonger where and when they were landed.

Organic Veggie Bake

D&P Byrne Organic Farm is beautifully located overlooking Skerries, just down the road from the gates of Ardgillan castle. Paddy's family has farmed in blackhills for four generations and he has more recently changed to completely organic, with free-range chickens and now an orchard too.

Ingredients

1.4kg Potatoes
350g Celeriac
500g Carrots
400g Pumpkin or Butternut Squash
200g Sweet Turnip
200g Parsnip
150g White Turnip
200g Kale
100g Onion or Leek
2 Cloves Garlic
1 Large Carrot (Grated)
1 Beetroot (Peeled and Grated)
Salt & Pepper

Method

Prep

Wash and peel the vegetables and pre-heat oven to 175°C.

In a large saucepan boil the potatoes and celeriac together, remove and mash.

Roughly chop your remaining vegetables (except onion/leek and garlic) and boil, on high heat, for 6 mins.

Drain and pour into an ovenproof baking dish.

Add your onion/leek, garlic and a pinch of salt.

Cover and place in the oven for 40 mins.

Uncover and spread your potato and celeriac mash over the roasted vegetable mix.

Cook for an additional 10 mins or until potatoes are golden brown.

To Plate

Remove from oven and leave to cool for 10 mins.

Serve with mixed greens topped with grated carrot & beetroot.

Paddy Byrne
I love the sea, shorelines and open streets of Skerries. The view from the farm is something I feel lucky to have.

Why Organic?

Organic production is a holistic system designed to optimize the productivity and fitness of
diverse communities within the agro-ecosystem, including soil organisms, plants, livestock and people. The principal goal of organic production is to develop enterprises that are sustainable and harmonious with the environment.

Check out www.organictrust.ie for more information on organic farming . . .

Baniza

LA BAKERY HAS A GREAT SELECTION OF FRESHLY-MADE CAKES AND DESSERTS. HERE, GALINA HAS TAKEN A TRADITIONAL BULGARIAN DISH (BANIZA) AND GIVEN IT HER OWN SKERRIES SAVOURY TWIST. BE CREATIVE HERE, ADD YOUR OWN INGREDIENTS AND PUT YOUR OWN TWIST ON THE DISH.

Ingredients

1 Filo Pastry (room temperature)
3 Large Eggs
300g Feta Cheese
3 Tbsp Natural Yoghurt
75g Melted Butter
1 Tbsp Soda or Baking Powder
Chopped Fresh Thyme

Method

Prep

Pre-heat oven to 200°C.

In a mixing bowl, crumble the cheese.

Add eggs, yoghurt and baking powder.

Mix well by hand or rubber spatula and set aside.

Butter the bottom and sides of a large square baking tray or dish (2 inches deep). Cover the bottom of the dish with 2 layers of filo pastry and brush with melted butter.

Spread a layer of the feta mixture and repeat the process until mixture and/or pastry is finished, making sure that the top of the dish is 6 buttered filo layers. Cut into even squares and sprinkle with chopped thyme.

Bake for approximately 35 mins or until golden brown.

To Plate

Remove from oven and let rest for about 5 minutes.

Serve warm with natural yoghurt on the side.

Jó étvágyat kívánunk!

Galina Koeva

Galina hails from Bulgaria and has lived in Ireland for 16 years, 5 of them in Skerries. Impressed by the stunning coastal walks, small boutique shops, great choice of pubs and spectacular restaurants, Galina and her family's decision to move to Skerries was easy. Galina's glowing pride in this small seaside town is proof that the community spirit and welcome of Skerries is there for all to experience and enjoy.

A QUAINT LITTLE TUCK SHOP OF ICE COLD DELIGHT
ON THEIR BEST BEHAVIOUR KIDS, WHEN THIS SHOP COMES INTO SIGHT,
BRING THE WHOLE FAMILY, AND DAD DON'T BE TIGHT!
MUCKY MESS! KINDA NUTS! MMM! BANOFFEE PIE,
OR WHAT ABOUT A LIGHTHOUSE?
HELP ME FIGURE WHAT I'LL TRY.
NO MATTER WHAT THE WEATHER
A COLD OR SUNNY DAY,
STORM IN A TEACUP WILL BE BUSY
MAKING LITTLE PEOPLE'S DAY

Crunchy Kinder Crêpes

We've all queued in the rain, wind and that one day of blistering sun to get our hands on an epic treat, a piping hot chocolate, tea or specialty coffee at **Storm in a Teacup**. This tiny shop of wonder proves to all that great things often do come in small packages!

Ingredients

Crêpe Mixture
125g Wheat Flour
2 Large Fresh Eggs
200ml Low-Fat Milk
1 Tsp Caster Sugar
1 Pinch Salt
1 Tbsp Sunflower Oil

Filling
4 Heaped Tbsp Chocolate Sauce
2 Kinder Bueno Wafer Bars
8 Large Pillow Marshmallows
Vanilla Ice Cream
Fresh Whipped Cream

Method

Prep
Sift the flour into a large mixing bowl. Beat eggs and milk together with salt and sugar. Whisk in gradually to the flour until mixture is of a smooth consistency. Leave to rest for 30 mins.
Crush Kinder Bueno bars and set aside.
Pour a little sunflower oil into a non-stick pan and add ¼ of the crêpe mix. Cook for 2 mins each side.
Gently heat your chocolate sauce in a bowl over some steaming water.
Plate up a crêpe and cover with a spoonful of chocolate sauce.
Sprinkle with crushed Kinders, add 2 marshmallows and fold.

Tip: be quick or it can get messy here!

To Plate
Decorate with icing sugar and serve with freshly whipped cream or vanilla ice cream . . . come on, you've come this far, why not both!?

Photo - Michael Flannery

Photo - Sharon O'Buachalla

Photo - Elaine McDonnell

Photo - Agnes Matthews

Family Recipe

Ingredients

Method

Notes

What's Happenin' Skerries!

A Guide to what goes on in Skerries during the year

There is loads to do in Skerries. Here are some of the big calendar events to look out for . . .
Check out www.visitskerries.ie for all the information you need on what to do and where in Skerries.

Summer

A festival for the whole family
Skerries Water Festival

The Street bike racing event of the year
Skerries 100 Road Races

An annual tradition in Skerries
The Raft Race

Filling our beautiful sea with sails
Sailing Club Regatta

Autumn

The town comes alive with music and culture
Soundwaves Festival

Our very own Wicker Man
Vintage Harvest Festival

Dress to impress
Skerries Rugby Club Fashion Show

Go out with a bang!
Fireworks Display at the Harbour

Winter

A Christmas treat for the kids
Santa at Skerries Mills

Raising loads of money for good causes
The Christmas Swim, BRR!

A thespian's dream
Skerries One Act Festival

Immerse yourself in the history of Skerries
Historical Society Miscellany

Spring

Thousands of goats line the streets
St. Patrick's Day Parade

Wheels and wheels
FBD Rás Street Party

Traditional music to delight
Skerries Trad Festival

The true meaning of community spirit
Darkness into Light

PHOTOS - IAN MURPHY

Winter

Razor Clams

One of the most frequently-caught shellfish in Skerries, these underrated molluscs make for a really delicious starter or main. Once regarded as a "Famine Food", jack-knife clams - as they're commonly known in the states - are now prized by oriental cooks and restaurants specialising in fish dishes.

Ingredients

8 Razor Clams
150g Pancetta or Smoked Bacon
Juice of ½ Lemon
1 Handful Fresh-Chopped Parsley
1 Clove Chopped Garlic
100g Grated Parmesan Cheese
30g Butter
Fresh Green Leaves

Method

Razor Clam Prep
Open the razor clams and remove the meat and clean out the shell.
Dice the clam meat and place in a bowl.
Roughly chop the pancetta or smoked bacon to the same size as the clam meat. Melt the butter and add to the mixture along with the garlic and parsley.
Mix together gently and add lemon juice, salt & pepper to taste.
Place the mixture back into the cleaned shells and sprinkle with the parmesan cheese.

To Plate
Place under a hot grill for 4-5 minutes and garnish with fresh greens.
Happy hunting!

Stephen Attley
Stephen is never far from the sea or kitchen. As a former head chef at Tarragon in Skerries and Octopussy's of Howth, Stephen's journey has truly taken him from pond to plate.

RED ISLAND
WINE Co.
Australia
Clare Valley
Riesling

Pan-Fried Seabass

A casual seafood restaurant located in the heart of Skerries, **Rockabill** has a chic, relaxed atmosphere that suits any occasion. An imaginative menu with some great specials on offer, and live music at the weekends to set the tone.

Ingredients

2 Seabass Fillets
6 Baby Potatoes
100g Green Beans
2 Sprigs Rosemary
2 Sprigs Thyme
2 Tbsp Olive Oil
2 Wedges Lemon
Sea Salt
Cracked Black Pepper

Method

Prep

Slice potatoes lengthways. In a bowl add the potatoes and season with salt, pepper, chopped rosemary, thyme and olive oil.
To a hot pan, add the potatoes and sauté (shallow fry) in sunflower oil for 10 mins or until golden brown.
Leave to stand for 5 mins.

The Fish

Score the seabass fillets on the skin sides, season with salt & cracked black pepper.
In a very hot pan, add olive oil and the seabass fillets skin side up for 1 min then turn over and cook for an additional 1 min.
Add green beans and finish under the grill for 1½ mins.

To Plate

Put sautéed potatoes in the middle of the plate and top with green beans. Finish with the seabass fillets.
Serve with a wedge of lemon.

Chris Grant

Head Chef
Chris has been working with food for over 17 years now. He is from the town and is well known for his exquisite fish dishes.

Chicken and Broccoli Bake

After hacking your way around Skerries Golf Club, nothing beats a nice pint and some tasty food at the 19th to help you forget about that three putt on the last. The clubhouse overlooks the 18th green, one of the best finishing parkland holes in Ireland.

Ingredients

4 Cubed Chicken Breasts
1 Large Broccoli
600ml Fresh Milk
50g Butter
50g Plain Flour
1 Tbsp Curry Powder
1 Tbsp Real Mayonnaise
50g Fresh Cream
50g Fresh Bread Crumbs
20g Grated Cheddar
1 Handful Chopped Parsley
1 Tbsp Coconut Oil
1 Chicken Stock Cube
Salt & Pepper
1 Tbsp Olive Oil

Method

Prep

Pre-heat the oven to 170°C.

Season the chicken with salt and pepper. Heat the coconut oil in a frying pan, cook the chicken over a medium heat and set aside.

Blanch the broccoli by placing into boiling salted water for 2-3 mins and plunge quickly into a bowl of ice-cold water.

For the Sauce

Add milk and stock cube to a saucepan and bring to the boil. Remove from heat. Meanwhile, in a separate saucepan, melt the butter.

When melted, add in the flour and cook over a medium heat for 4-5 mins.

When smooth, gradually add in the hot milk and cook over a gentle heat for a further 4-5 mins. Add in the curry powder, mayonnaise and fresh cream.

The Crust

Mix the fresh bread crumbs, cheddar, parsley, olive oil, salt and pepper. In a casserole dish mix the chicken and broccoli and cover with the sauce. Mix well and cover with the crust.

Bake in the pre-heated oven for 25-30 mins.

Karl Rogers

I have been looking after the catering in Skerries Golf Club for the last eleven years. I moved to Skerries fourteen years ago after marrying local girl Mary Beggs. I settled in Skerries very quickly (even though I was a half-shirt from Balbriggan!) and I was always made feel very welcome in the community.

PHOTOS – ANTHONY HAND

Skerries Golf Club
Est. 1905

A great parkland course that provides magnificent panoramic views of the Irish Sea and coastline, extending from the Mountains of Mourne all the way to Howth. It is a welcoming club with great green fee rates and with some really tough closing holes!

The Smokey Dog Burger

The Salty Dog is a homely bar and bistro with a quirky, artistic and cosy décor. This, coupled with Ray and Catherine's love for local Irish music, is the experience and vision they would like to share with everyone. The wings are great and their burgers are very popular.

Ingredients

Burger
340g Lean Mince Beef
2 Sesame Baps
2 Pinch Salt & Pepper
2 Tsp Worcestershire Sauce
2 Slices Irish Smoked Cheddar
Fresh Iceberg lettuce

Crispy Onions
350ml Sunflower Oil
2 Small Onions (sliced thinly)
125ml Buttermilk
60g Plain Flour
Salt & Pepper

BBQ Sauce
50ml Ketchup
100ml Water
2 tsp Balsamic Vinegar
125g Light Muscovado Sugar
75g Caster Sugar
½ Tsp Onion Powder
½ Tsp Ground Mustard
2 Tsp Lemon Juice
Fresh Ground Black Pepper
4 Tbsp Worcestershire Sauce

Method

For the Burger
In a mixing bowl add the mince, salt, pepper and Worcestershire sauce. Combine well and separate into two patties. Set aside and refrigerate for 15 mins.

BBQ Sauce
In a medium saucepan, combine all of your ingredients. Bring to a boil and reduce heat to a simmer uncovered. Stir frequently for 45 mins.

Crispy Onions
Soak the onions in the buttermilk for at least 30 mins.
In a medium saucepan heat the sunflower oil.
In a bowl combine flour with salt and pepper.
Using one hand for wet ingredients and one had for dry, take a handful of onion from the buttermilk and immediately dunk into the flour mixture. Coat well with your dry hand and shake off the excess. Fry the onions 1-2 mins each side until crispy and golden. Be careful not to stack onions while frying, helping to prevent them sticking together. Set aside the onion rings on a paper towel.

To Plate
Cook your burgers under a hot grill or on the barbeque.
About 5 minutes each side should do. Top the burgers with smoked cheddar and melt the cheese under the grill while lightly toasting the baps. Layer the burgers with BBQ sauce, lettuce and crispy onions.

Tip: Have some napkins to hand, it might get messy!

Fish Pie

Great live music every weekend at **Raff's on the Corner**, and right in the middle of the town. Great choice for kids on the menu, with an inviting atmosphere. The amber door has some great steak offers, with loads of space for large groups.

Ingredients

1 Leek (thinly sliced)
2 Carrots (peeled and diced)
500g Mashed Potato
150g Cod
150g Smoked Haddock
150g Salmon
60g Butter
2 Tbsp Plain Flour
500ml Fresh Milk
50g Grated Cheddar
2 Tbsp Olive Oil
Salt & Pepper

Method

Prep

Pre-heat oven to 180°C.

In a hot pan, fry the leeks and carrots for 3-4 mins.

Dice the fish into 5cm cubed bites. In an ovenproof dish, add the fish, cooked leeks and carrots and set aside.

Sauce

In a saucepan, heat the milk gently.

In a separate pan, melt the butter on a medium heat, then add flour and stir vigorously for 2 mins. Gradually add the heated milk. Simmer on a low heat for 5 minutes. Remove from heat and allow to stand for 1 minute. Stir in the grated cheddar cheese. Season to taste.

To Bake

In an ovenproof dish, pour the mixture over the fish and vegetables. Cover with mashed potato and bake in the oven for 35 mins.

Jimmy and Mary Rafferty

Owners, Raff's on the Corner

Don't visit Skerries without coming along to Raff's on the Corner, where you can enjoy the best in Irish Hospitality! Let Us Entertain You!

Szechuan Chicken with Rice

CHOPSTICKS IS ONE OF THE QUICKEST TAKEAWAY SERVICES IN SKERRIES WITH FRIENDLY STAFF AND WHOPPER PORTIONS. THIS IS A GEM OF A RESTAURANT. WE'VE SEEN THE HEAD CHEF IN ACTION AND WE CHALLENGE ANYONE TO TRY AND KEEP UP WITH HIS WOK SKILLS. GREAT FOOD EVERY TIME.

Ingredients

500g Chicken Breast (cubed)
1 Chopped Red Pepper
1 Medium Onion (chopped)
2 Tbsp Dark Soya Sauce
1 Tbsp Cider Vinegar
½ Tsp Smoked Paprika
(harissa powder or chilli flakes)
2 Tbsp Corn Flour
3 Spring Onion (diagonally sliced)
3 Cloves Garlic (diced small)
60ml Water
1 Tsp Caster Sugar
1 Tbsp Sesame Oil

Method

Prep
In a bowl, mix together the cornflour and cubed chicken breast.
Heat the sesame oil in a hot pan and fry the chicken over medium heat.
Add the peppers, paprika, onion & garlic and cook until golden brown.
Next add the soy sauce, vinegar, water and sugar.
Cover and reduce to a simmer for 4-5 mins or until the chicken is cooked. Add the spring onion and heat for 1 minute.

To Plate
Serve over basmati or jasmin rice.

The Year of the Goat

Ok, so there are the Skerries Goats, but if you were born in these years, then you really are a Goat:
1919, 31, 43, 55, 67, 79, 91, 2003, 2015. People born in a year of the Goat are generally believed to be gentle, mild-mannered, stable, sympathetic, amicable, and brimming with a strong sense of kindheartedness and justice. According to Chinese astrology, each animal zodiac has its own lucky numbers, days, colours, flowers, and a best direction!
Here are the Goat's: Lucky numbers: 2, 7, Lucky days: 7th and 30th, Lucky colors: green, red, and purple.
Lucky flowers: carnations and primroses, Lucky direction: north

Shin Beef - Osso Bucco

Dessie, as he's known to his customers, has been a butcher in Skerries for over 50 years. Here with a less mainstream (but no less delicious) cut of meat is an Italian special that will warm your cockles. Buy the cut of meat with the bone still on.

Ingredients

2kg Shin Beef (plus bone)
3 Tbsp Plain Flour
3 Carrots (peeled batons)
2 Onions (thinly-sliced)
3 Cloves Garlic (thinly-sliced)
1 Red Chilli (thinly-sliced)
½ Jar of Passata
1 Sprig Thyme
4 Sage Leaves
1 Bay Leaf
220ml Beef Stock
½ Bottle of Red Wine
Salt and Pepper

Method

Prep
Dust the beef in seasoned flour. In a large frying pan with hot oil, brown all sides of the beef and transfer to a casserole dish.
Lower the heat and cook the carrots, onions, chilli and garlic in the frying pan until soft.

The Stew
Deglaze the pan with the wine. Rapidly simmer, making sure to scrape and remove the floury residues. When the smell of alcohol has evaporated pour the mixture into the pot. Add the passata, beef stock and herbs.
On a very low heat setting, cook for a minimum 3-4 hours, uncovered. Check the meat as you go along. You'll know it's cooked when you no longer need a knife to cut the meat and it falls apart easily.

Tip: Preparing this dish the day before and reheating helps to intensify the flavours.

Osso Bucco

Literally means "Bones with Holes". It originates from Northern Italy and has always been made using local wine and herbs. This dish is rich, delicate and absolutely delicious. Serve up with your favourite potato. Stoke the fire, light a few candles and pour a large glass of red wine. Godere!

RED ISLAND
WINE Co.

Barbera
D'Alba or D'Asti
Italy

A Skerries Christmas

Here, we've put together our very own special Goat's Cheese Christmas feast -
Turkey and Ham with all the trimmings! Christmas is a time for family and friends and The Goat's Cheese wouldn't be complete without an homage to our favourite time of year.

TIP: REMEMBER TO COOK YOUR TURKEY IN SMALL DISH. DON'T LEAVE TOO MUCH ROOM AROUND THE BIRD OR YOU RISK BURNING OFF THE JUICES. YOU'LL NEED THESE FOR THE GRAVY.

RED ISLAND WINE Co.
PINOT NOIR
OTAGO - NZ

The Bird
Ingredients

6-7kg Farm-Fresh Turkey
(approx. 14-16lbs)
1 Bunch Thyme
½ Bunch Rosemary
½ Bunch Sage
1 Lemon (cut in half)
1 Large Onion (cut into quarters)
1 Length Butcher's Twine
125ml Melted Butter
Roasting Thermometer

Method

Prep

Preheat oven to 200°C for 20 minutes before cooking.

Melt the butter with ½ bunch of your thyme, remove from the heat and set aside to cool. Wearing a plastic glove, work the herb butter under the skin covering the breasts. Keep some of the mixture for brushing the turkey at the halfway point of cooking.

Dry the inside of the turkey with a paper towel and stuff with the remaining ingredients. Tie the legs together gently with butcher's twine. Tying too tightly risks the legs not cooking enough at the joint. Rub the turkey with the remaining butter mixture and place onto a baking tray breast side down. Take wing tips and pull them up onto the bird, they should be pointing at each other. Bake for 1 hour. Next, reduce heat to 175°C and bake for an additional hour.

After the 2nd hour is up flip the bird and insert the roasting thermometer into the thickest part of the thigh. Brush the turkey with the remaining herb butter and return to bake until cooked. The final temperature needs to reach 75-77°C.

To Plate

When cooked remove from the oven, cover with aluminium foil and let rest for 1 hour. Reserve the drippings for the Turkey gravy (see page 71). Carve and it's time for Christmas Crackers!!!

Tips: Stuffing your turkey will affect the cooking time. This will add time in the oven and could dry out your turkey. We like crispy stuffing and a roasting tray works great. Keep it separate and cook a day in advance.

If your turkey looks like it's going to burn or getting too dark, press a sheet of aluminium foil over the top of the bird, but don't wrap it up.

It is important that you do not open the oven while cooking. By opening the door of the oven, you're dropping the temperature too quickly and risk drying your bird out in the process. Be patient, a quality bird is worth it!

 Serves: 6-8   Cook/Prep Time: 50 mins

Brussel Sprouts with Pancetta & Walnuts

Ingredients

½ kg Brussel Sprouts
60g Chopped Pancetta
1 Red Onion (thinly-sliced)
100g Chopped Walnuts
1 Tbsp Olive Oil
Salt & Pepper to Taste

Method

Prep

Rinse, wash and peel away any discoloured leaves from the sprouts. Preheat oven to 190°C.

In a hot pan, cook the red onion, pancetta and walnuts on medium heat until onion is glossed and walnuts are toasted.

In an ovenproof dish add the brussel sprouts, olive oil, salt and pepper. Bake for 30 mins.

Next, add the pancetta, red onion and walnut mix and bake for an additional 10-15 mins until cooked and tender.

 Serves: 6-8   Cook/Prep Time: 50 mins

Honey-Roasted Carrot & Parsnip

Ingredients

8 Large Carrots Peeled
8 Large Parsnip Peeled
8 Tsp Butter
8 Sprig Fresh Thyme
Honey
Sea Salt

Method

Prep

Preheat oven to 200°C.

In tin foil place 1 tsp butter, 1 sprig of thyme, 1 carrot and 1 parsnip. Drizzle with a little honey and wrap tightly with your foil. Do this with the remaining carrots & parsnips.

Place in oven and bake for 40 mins. Check to see if cooked, using a sharp knife. When cooked, the knife will easily pierce into the veg. Keep wrapped until plating up.

To Plate

Cut into even batons and serve with the main course.

Serves: 6-8    Cook/Prep Time: 2 hours

Honey & Herb Irish Glazed Ham

Ingredients

3.75kg Ham (half bone-in ham)
Cloves
Glaze
125 ml Tullamore Dew Whiskey
3 Tbsp Honey
3 Tbsp Muscovado Sugar
1 Tbsp Cider Vinegar
1 Tbsp Rosemary (finely-chopped)

Method

Prep
Preheat oven to 150°C.
Trim the excess fat and silver (tough bits) from your ham, leaving an even amount of fat around the meat. Next, score the fat using a sharp knife into a diamond pattern. Press cloves into the cross cuts.
Do not cut into the ham itself. Place in a roasting dish in the middle of your oven, fat side down.
The Glaze
In a saucepan, simmer the whiskey until reduced by half. Remove from heat and allow to cool. Combine all ingredients in a bowl and mix well.
Applying the Glaze
After an hour cooking the ham, start applying the glaze. Brush the ham quickly, every 15 mins, keeping it moist. Add water or chicken stock to prevent the bottom of the pan burning during this process. Remove the ham when cooked, reglaze and let stand for 15 mins.
ESTIMATED COOKING TIME: 15 MINS PER ½ KG WITH AN INTERNAL TEMPERATURE OF APPROXIMATELY 65°C

Serves: 6-8   Cook/Prep Time: 50 mins

Crispy Roast Potatoes

Ingredients

1.5kg Maris Piper Potatoes
3 Tbsp Duck or Goose Fat
2 Sprigs Rosemary
4 Whole Cloves Garlic (not peeled)

Method

Prep
Preheat oven to 190°C.
Peel and cut the potatoes into evenly-sized quarters.
Boil potatoes for 10 mins. Remove and toss in a colander, roughing up the edges for perfect crispy roast potatoes.
Place all the ingredients into an ovenproof roasting dish and mix well.
Roast for 30 mins until golden in colour, mixing again after 20 mins.
TIP: BOIL THE POTATOES THE DAY BEFORE. PREP FOR ROASTING AND COVER UNTIL TIME TO BAKE.

Turkey Gravy

Ingredients

Reserved Turkey Drippings
230g Plain Flour
1 Tsp Fresh Ground Black Pepper
Salt and Pepper to Taste
Chicken Stock
(add to drippings to make 1 litre)

Method

Prep

Remove the turkey from the pan and pour the drippings through a fine sieve. Set aside for 5 mins. When the fat settles to the top, spoon 3 scoops into your turkey roasting pan. Discard the remaining fat from the drippings. Add the chicken stock to the drippings until you have 1 litre of liquid.

Using a whisk, gradually add the flour to the fat in the pan and cook over low heat stirring constantly. Stir well until all the turkey bits form a smooth bubbling mixture.

Remove from heat and gradually stir in your litre of liquid. Return to heat and stir continuously, bringing the gravy to the boil. Cook until gravy thickens.

Add salt and pepper to taste.

  Serves: 6-8   Cook/Prep Time: 50 mins

Apricot and Sage Stuffing

Ingredients

3 Large White Onions
8 Dried Apricots (finely-sliced)
3 Cups Fresh Bread Crumbs
3 Tbsp Dried Sage
2 Tbsp apple sauce
2 Tbsp Olive Oil
1½ Tsp Salt
½ Tsp Pepper

Method

Prep

Place the apricots in warm water to soak for 10 minutes, while you prepare the rest of the stuffing ingredients.

Stuffing

Boil a pan of water and place the peeled, whole onions in. Simmer for 8 minutes, then drain.

Finely-chop the onions, and place in a large bowl.

Add the apricots to the bowl of onions along with the remaining ingredients. Mix everything together well and place in a lightly greased 8×8 inch baking-pan, spreading evenly.

Bake in preheated oven at 200°C for 30-40 minutes until browned and crispy. Serve with the works!

Gluten-Free Mince Pies

Let's face it, christmas just wouldn't be christmas without mince pies. And yes, they're an indulgent treat, but all the more reason to bake up a batch for visiting family and friends. From **Janet Weldon**, Here's a gluten-free, coeliac-friendly way to feel a little less guilty about eating half the plate!

Ingredients

Mincemeat
Grated Zest of 1 Lemon
1 Banana (mashed)
70ml Fresh Orange Juice
1 Pinch of Grated Nutmeg
1 Pinch of Allspice
1 Tsp Ground Cinnamon
2 Tbsp Golden Syrup
170g Raisins
80g Dried Apricots
80g Dried Sour Cherries
80g Dried Cranberries
80g Dried Blueberries
2 Tbsp Brandy (optional)

Pastry
130g Plain Flour (gluten-free)
40g Ground Almonds
60g Icing Sugar
2 Egg Yolks (cold water if needed)
1 Tsp Vanilla Essence
1 Tsp Xanthan Gum
110g Real Butter (cold)
1 Egg (beaten)
100ml Milk

Method

For the Mincemeat
Mix all the ingredients well into a bowl and leave covered in the fridge overnight for the flavours to develop.

Pastry
Sieve flour, icing sugar and xanthan gum into a large mixing bowl. Dice the hard butter. Add to the sieved ingredients and break mixture down with cold fingertips, until the mixture feels like fine breadcrumbs.
Add the ground almonds, egg yolks, vanilla essence and enough cold water to bring mixture together by hand. Roll into single portion bowls, wrap in cling film and refrigerate to chill for 20 mins (it's important not to handle the mixture too much, don't melt the butter).
Pre-heat oven to 180°C.
Sprinkle worktop with gluten free flour and roll the pastry thin.
Cut with a scone cutter or ring and place in a muffin/bun tin.
Fill each with 1½ tsp of mincemeat. Roll out remaining pastry and cut the circles. Brush water around edges of exposed pastry in your tin and press the cut circle lids on top. Brush the tops with beaten egg and milk. Bake for 20-30 mins or until golden brown.

Tip: Mince Pies freeze very well!

Chocolate & Peanut Butter Mousse with fresh Raspberries & Salted Caramel Popcorn

Although he's not based in Skerries now, **Colin Kelly** was an obvious choice to be included in our book. With this spectacular dessert, we're sure you'll agree he didn't let us down.

Ingredients

Mousse
240ml Double Cream
170g Dark Chocolate (66%)
3 Tbsp Smooth Peanut Butter
4 Eggs
4 Tbsp Caster Sugar

Salted Caramel
175g Soft Brown Sugar
(light muscovado)
300ml Cream
50g Butter
½ tsp Salt

Caramel Popcorn
100ml Salted Caramel (see above)
Popcorn
Toasted Chopped Peanuts
Fresh Raspberries

Method

Prep
Melt the chocolate and peanut butter in a bowl over simmering water until smooth. Whisk cream until soft peaks form.
Whisk sugar and eggs over warm water until foamy and slightly coloured. Fold this mixture into the chocolate mix.
Using a rubber spatula fold in the whipped cream.
Allow to set in a serving dish or container for 2 hours.

Salted Caramel
In a flat bottom pot, warm and stir the sugar until you have a golden syrup. Stir in the butter. Add the cream slowly, whisking continuously and add the salt. Reserve a small amount for garnish.

Caramel Popcorn
Pre-heat the oven to 180°C.
Lightly toast the peanuts for 5-8 minutes on a baking tray.
Warm the caramel in a pot.
Add the popcorn and toasted peanuts and mix until everything is covered well with caramel.
Empty onto a cooling rack or sheet of greaseproof paper.

To Plate
Using a tablespoon, spread some reserved caramel along the centre of the plate. Then using a large warm spoon, form the mousse into a quenelle on the centre of the plate.
Randomly place caramelised popcorn and fresh raspberries around the mousse.
Finish with finely-grated chocolate.
Salty sweet awesomeness to share with a loved one!

Colin Kelly

Colin's culinary journey started in the Windmill in Skerries where he started as a kitchen porter. There he quickly discovered kitchen life was his calling. He went on to work in some of Dublin and London's top end establishments including head chef at the award winning One Pico restaurant for 4 years.

Goat's Cheese and Blueberry Mousse

One of Skerries' oldest and best known food destinations, **The Red Bank,** is a classical guest house and restaurant - fine dining personified. As a special treat for The Goat's Cheese, The Red Bank have perfected a smooth, rich and creamy dessert using goat's cheese. Enjoy!

Ingredients

1L Whipping Cream
150g Soft Goats Cheese
1 Tbsp Caster Sugar
500g Blueberries
125ml Dry White Wine
4 Leaves Gelatine

Equipment

Electric mixer w/ bowl
Large Mixing Bowl
6 Ramekin (or cups)
Cling Film

Summer Berry Sauce

60g Cranberries
60g Raspberries
60g Blackberries
60g Blueberries
250ml Dry White Wine
2 Tbsp Castor Sugar

Method

Prep

Heat the white wine and add blueberries to poach until bursting. Pass through sieve pressing until you extract all flesh but for skins. (If you prefer the roughage, liquidise everything in a blender).

Add the gelatine leaves to the warm blueberries and allow the gelatine to dissolve by stirring. Place the blueberry mix and bowl into a larger container with Iced water to speed the cooling to about 5°C. Keep a close eye stirring the deep coloured liquid as it sets, do not allow to fully set as you need to pour it into the next bowl.

In a large mixing bowl, whisk 750ml of cream with the sugar until peaks can be formed. Empty into a separate bowl and set aside. No need to clean the whisking bowl yet.

Add the goat's cheese into the whisking bowl and add the remaining cream. Beat until the cheese and cream are soft.

Check the flavour — it should be slightly sweet but with a tart, tangy taste from the goat's cheese.

Add the cooled blueberry liquid and beat.

Line the ramekins with the cling film. Pour in the mixture and place in the fridge for 4 hours.

Summer Berry Sauce

Dissolve the sugar in the wine by warming, then add the berries and poach until all are very soft. Allow to cool.

When the ramekins are set after 4 hours, turn out onto plates removing the cling film. Drizzle the summer berry sauce around the mousse & serve.

RIESLING

The Legend of St. Patrick's Footprint

Hugh Fitzgerald Ryan

There is always water in Saint Patrick's footprint, even at the lowest tide. This enables you to make a wish, but, of course, you must never tell anyone what that wish is. I have made a good many wishes there since my father first showed it to me a long time ago. I recall him holding my left hand and lowering me down, to dip my fingers in the water and whisper the wish to myself and to Patrick.

I can only conclude that a great many of those wishes came true, but I can't remember them all. I didn't make one yesterday, because my footing was precarious on the wet seaweed and there was nobody there to hold my hand. I had no wish either to inadvertently join the intrepid winter swimmers of Skerries, the aptly named Frosties.

It is no surprise that a man of the stature of Patrick should have made such an impression. There can be no argument about the fact that his arrival was the most significant thing that ever happened in Skerries or indeed, in Ireland. There will be arguments, of course. Scholars argue. Was Patrick a Gaul, a Briton, or a Welshman? Was he Patrick at all, or just somebody else called Patrick? Legends have grown up around him. He made a giant leap from his island and landed so forcefully on the rock at Red Island that his footprint remained in the stone. I prefer that version to the more prosaic suggestion that the people marked the spot where he set foot on the mainland of Ireland to begin his mission. That is an awesome thought: fifteen hundred and eighty two years ago, a man arrived from far away to preach the Gospel to the people who had held him in his boyhood as a slave.

The story is told that Julius Caesar, as a young man, was held for ransom, by Cilician pirates. It is likely that they enjoyed his company. He was noted for his 'people skills', but he promised that he would return some day and crucify them all. No doubt they laughed at his joke. He kept his promise. Patrick made the obverse of Caesar's promise. He came without legions or fleet. He saw. He conquered Ireland. Who was the better man? There's a subject for an argument. What legend can adequately express such courage? His leap took him from the island on the right, Inis Phádraig, to a point beside the white wall on the left. It is still a world record. You may stand in his footprint but you could never fill his shoes. His name went out from this point and scattered 'like a wildflower' all over Ireland and all over the world, wherever Irish people have settled. His image is everywhere.

Look closely at the ruined monastery on his island, Inis Phádraig, and you will see a white, ghostly figure in the window, the Bishop's Window. It is the man himself, every inch a bishop.

Go and make a wish at his footprint, but be sure to get someone to hold your hand . . .

WITH THANKS TO HUGH FITZGERALD RYAN
READ HUGH'S BLOG HERE – WWW.HFRYAN.WORDPRESS.COM

Photo - Markbroderickie

Poached Salmon and Apple

Seasons, NESTLED BESIDE THE MONUMENT, SERVE SUBLIME FRESH BREAKFAST, KNOCK-OUT CAKES, TREATS AND GREAT COFFEE. MEL, THE OWNER, IS A REALLY WELCOMING HOST AND THE STAFF ECHO HER CHARM. THERE'S A LARGE AREA UPSTAIRS WITH GREAT VIEWS AND BIG ROOMY TABLES . . .

Ingredients

500g Salmon Fillet
1 Bay Leaf
5 Peppercorns
1 Pinch Sea Salt
50g Butter
125g Red Apple (peeled & cubed)
115g Smoked Salmon (diced)
5g Chopped Parsley
100g Mascarpone
1 Pomegranate
Llewellyn's Apple Syrup
Organic Leaves

Method

Prep
Poach the salmon in boiling salted water with the bay leaf and peppercorns for 10 mins. Remove and cool.

Production
In a saucepan, melt the butter and add the peeled and cubed apple. Heat apple for 3 mins, glossed but still firm (al dente). Add the smoked salmon and cook for 1 min. Remove and cool.
Flake the salmon into a mixing bowl. Add the parsley and apple mix. Gently fold by hand.
Shape or press into dish or ring and refrigerate for 20 mins or until firm. Spread a little mascarpone on top and portion.

To Plate
Decorate each plate with pomegranate seeds, dots of Llewellyn's Apple Syrup and garnish with organic leaves.

PHOTO DANIEL GEESON

Country Vegetable Soup with Brown Bread

THE WATERMILL CAFÉ, UPSTAIRS AT THE SKERRIES MILLS, IS A WONDERFUL LITTLE COFFEE SHOP. SINCE THE 12TH CENTURY FLOUR HAS BEEN MILLED AT THIS VERY UNIQUE LOCATION. THERE THEY BAKE THEIR BROWN BREAD DAILY, USING ONLY THE FRESHEST INGREDIENTS. NOW YOU CAN TOO!

Ingredients

Soup
1 Medium Onion
1 Potato
2 Carrots
1 Leek
2 Celery Sticks
1 Parsnip
1 Small Cauliflower
1 Small Broccoli
50g Butter
Olive Oil
500ml Vegetable Stock
80ml Cooking Cream
2 Sprigs Parsley
Salt and Pepper

Brown Bread
250g Stone Ground Soft Flour
250g Wholemeal Flour
1 Tsp Salt
1 Tsp Bread Soda
25g Margarine
350ml Buttermilk

Method

Country Vegetable Soup
Roughly chop all the vegetables. In a large saucepan heat the butter and oil. Add the onion and potato and cook on medium to high heat until onions are translucent.
Add the remaining vegetables and stock. Bring to a boil then reduce to a simmer until the vegetables are cooked. Remove saucepan from stovetop onto a heatproof surface. With a hand blender, blitz the mixture to your required consistency. Return saucepan to the stovetop and add the cream. Reheat to a light simmer until cream is fully incorporated.
Season with salt and pepper to taste.

TIP: GARNISH EACH SOUP BOWL WITH A DRIZZLE OF FRESH CREAM AND SPRIG OF PARSLEY.

Brown Bread
Pre-heat oven to 180°C. Oil your loaf tin and dust with flour. Mix the dry ingredients in a large bowl. Add the margarine and work the mixture gently by hand adding small amounts of buttermilk until completely incorporated.
Take care not to overwork the mixture. Don't let is get too wet or too dry either. The dough should be nice and soft. Dust your work surface with plain flour and turn out the mixture onto it. Shape into a loaf and place in your tin. Slash the top of the loaf lengthways with a sharp knife.
Bake for 45-50 mins checking frequently near the end of the baking time to ensure it is cooked.

St. Patrick's Purse

Chef **Terry McCoy** is Skerries' very own not-so-secret culinary weapon. A well respected and award winning chef who has become famous across Ireland for his mastery of food. Here, inspired by our very own Saint Patrick, is Terry's take on a Goat's Cheese Parcel.

Ingredients

250g Soft Goat's Cheese
(Boilie Fivemiletown)
1 Apple (peeled and grated)
1 Egg Beaten with 2 Tbsp Cream
(egg wash)
Black Pepper
2 Sheets Rice Paper
Mixed Green Leaves
Dressing or Vinaigrette

Method

Production
Preheat oven to 190°C.
Brush one sheet of rice paper with the egg wash, place the goat's cheese and grated apple in the centre & fold up into a square-shaped parcel.
Place the parcel in the centre of the 2nd sheet of rice paper and gather up the sides into a round shape.
Twist the edges together on the top (like the historic purse that Saint Patrick himself might have used!). Brush with the egg wash & bake at 190°C for 15-20 mins.

To Plate
To your mixed greens, add the dressing and place your golden baked parcel in the middle.

St. Patrick's Island
The Island known locally as "Inis Pádraig" or Church Island is almost inaccessible so it is one of the least-visited church sights in Ireland. The remains of the church, raided by the Vikings in 789 AD, can be seen from Red Island. Keep an eye out on St. Patrick's Day for the traditional "greening" of the island...

RED ISLAND WINE Cº
Portugal
•Douro / Alentejo•

Aidan's

Believed to be the longest-serving single-use shop in the town of Skerries, opening in 1906. The shop name above the door still says John Fox, who built the shop over 100 years ago.

Our family took over in September 1989 and are still going strong, says Aidan.

Between the 3 full-time butchers, Aidan, Aidan Junior and Damian Barker, there is nearly a combined century of expertise, covering every aspect of dressing and preparing meats.

Roast Rack of Lamb Rub

AIDAN'S BUTCHER BY THE MONUMENT IS A BRILLIANT LITTLE VICTUALLER WITH EVERYTHING YOU NEED. ALWAYS A FRIENDLY SMILE TO GREET THEIR HUNGRY CUSTOMERS, AND HUGE SUPPORTERS OF THE LOCAL COMMUNITY. THESE GUYS KNOW THEIR MEAT!

Ingredients

6 Chop Rack of Lamb
(ask your local butcher)
2 Tbsp Olive Oil
3 Cloves Garlic
1 Stem Rosemary
Salt & Pepper

Method

Garlic & Rosemary Rub

In a food processor, blitz together garlic, rosemary & olive oil for 20 seconds.

Roast Lamb

Preheat oven to 180°C. Rub the lamb with salt and peper. Place lamb on top oven rack and cook for 20 mins. Next, remove from oven and work the rub into the fat of the lamb. Take care, the meat will be hot! Turn over and return to oven, for an additional 20 mins, cooking each side to medium-rare.

For roast potatoes see page 70

For honey-roasted carrot and parsnip see page 69

TIP: COOK FOR AN ADDITIONAL 10 MINS FOR MEDIUM-TO-WELL DONE.

Pan-Seared Hake with Chorizo Crust

You'll find **Brasco's** at the top of the harbour road. Its magnificent views of the harbour make it worth the trip alone, but the food, thankfully, is very special too. Pierre is a fantastic chef and is a master with seafood.

Ingredients

500g Hake
200g Cannellini Beans
800g Chicken Stock
1 Sprig Chopped Rosemary
120g Melted Butter
400g Baby Potatoes
1 Tsp Salt
200g Chopped Chorizo
160g Bread Crumbs

Pesto
50g Basil
20g Parmesan
50g Olive Oil
20g Pine Nuts
1 Clove Garlic

Method

Pesto
In a food processor, blitz together basil, parmesan, olive oil, pine nuts and garlic.

Cannellini Bean Purée
In a medium saucepan, simmer 140g of cannellini beans with chicken stock, rosemary and butter for 20 mins. Blitz with food processor.

Cannellini Bean Emulsion
In a small saucepan, add 60g of cannellini beans, 60g of chopped chorizo and 2 tsp butter. Simmer on a low heat to emulsify. Put the emulsion on top of the purée.

Chorizo Crust
In a food processor, blitz together 140g chorizo, bread crumbs and melted butter. Spread the mix between 2 baking parchments.

Baby Boiled Potatoes
In a saucepan, boil potatoes for 10 minutes or until cooked. Crush and season with butter and salt.

Pan-Seared Hake
Pan-fry the hake with the skin side down. Half-cook then place on an ovenproof baking tray and top with the chorizo crust. Preheat oven to 180°C and bake for 5 mins.

To Plate
Spread the cannellini bean purée around the plate. Add crushed baby potatoes to the middle then drizzle the basil pesto around the plate. Place the hake on top of the potatoes with the chorizo crust facing upwards. Serve and enjoy.

Pierre Pratt
Head chef
Pierre acquired his passion for creating and inspiring dishes in his native France. He refined his skills working in his hometown in South Western France for 8 years. He came to Brasco's in 2016 and owners Paul and Stephen are delighted to have someone with his skill set and passion involved.

A WHITE RIOJA

RED ISLAND WINE CO.

Chicken and Mushroom Risotto

Di Vino is a family run Italian Restaurant situated behind the church, right in the heart of Skerries. They serve modern, authentic italian food and wine in a cosy and friendly atmosphere. The service is always excellent too which only adds to its charm . . .

Ingredients

4 Chicken Breasts
100g Dried Porcini Mushrooms
1 Tsp Truffle Oil
1 Shallot (finely-diced)
1L Veg/Chicken Stock (2 cubes)
250g Arborio Rice (Carnaroli)
Olive Oil
50g Butter
100ml White Wine
50g Fresh Grated Parmesan
Salt & Pepper to taste

Method

Prep
Ahead of time, soak the dried porcini mushrooms in cold water for 30 mins. Drain when softened.

Pan-Seared & Baked Chicken
Pre-heat oven to 190°C. In a hot pan, add a generous amount of olive oil to a medium heat. Add the chicken breasts and cook until golden brown on each side (approx. 2 mins per side). Place into oven and bake for 20 mins.

Porcini Risotto
Important: Remeber to stir continuously and gently throughout this process with a wooden spoon to help release the natural starches in the rice. This will ensure the ingredients do not burn and stick to your pan and your risotto is smooth and creamy.

Production
In a large saucepan, heat 2 tbsp olive oil. Add the shallot and fry for 2 mins. Add the porcini mushrooms and cook for 3 mins. Add the arborio rice. Cook for 3 mins or until rice is glossed. Pour in the wine and cook for 3 mins until liquid is absorbed/evaporated. Add vegetable stock 2 oz at a time, remember to stir, and allow liquid to absorb. Continue this process (approx. 20 mins) until all of the vegetable stock is absorbed. Add a little hot water if rice is undercooked. Remove from heat and stir in the butter. Stir fast and continuously until butter is absorbed. Finally, add the fresh grated parmesan and stir. Add salt & pepper to taste.

To Plate
Divide risotto onto 4 plates and top with the cooked chicken breast. Drizzle each plate with a little truffle oil and enjoy!

Tip: Keep your vegetable stock hot. Risotto is always worth the work!

Pan-Seared Cod wrapped in Parma Ham

OLLIES PLACE IS WELL KNOWN FOR ITS WEEKEND NIGHTLIFE, BUT THEY ALSO DO GREAT LUNCH SPECIALS THAT ARE EXCELLENT VALUE. A BRIGHT AND CHEERFUL SPOT, WITH FRIENDLY STAFF AND A DELICIOUS RANGE OF FOOD. COCKTAILS ARE A MUST!

Ingredients

500g Cod
4 Slices Parma Ham
500g Pre-Boiled Baby Potatoes
½ Red Pepper (roughly-chopped)
½ Tbsp Olive Oil (sunflower oil)
1 Onion (finely-diced)
1 Clove Garlic (crushed)
2 Tbsp Butter
2 Sprigs Thyme
½ Glass White Wine
2 Tbsp White Wine Vinegar
½ Cup Cooking Cream
1 Small Handful Capers
Salt & Pepper

Method

Potato & Red Pepper
Boil the baby potatoes ahead of time and leave to cool.
In a hot pan, add sliced potatoes and chopped red pepper. Add 1 tbsp butter and salt & pepper. Cook for 6-7 mins and stir occasionally to avoid burning.

White Wine Cream Sauce
In a medium saucepan, melt 1 tbsp butter and add chopped onions, garlic, thyme and simmer for 2-3 mins. Add white wine and vinegar and reduce by half. Add cream and simmer until sauce thickens.
Add capers and salt & pepper to taste.

Pan-Seared Cod
Cut the cod into two equal portions. Prepare each portion of cod, laying flat 2 slices of parma ham (slightly overlapping) lengthways.
Place both portions of cod on parma ham and wrap snugly.
Pre-heat oven to 180°C.
Heat a pan on medium heat and add olive oil. Place cod into the pan and cook for 2 mins each side, then into the oven for 8 mins.

Plating Up
Place the potato & peppers in a large bowl, top with your baked cod, pour over the cream sauce and enjoy!

Bombay House Korma Special

BOMBAY HOUSE, LOCATED ON STRAND STREET, IS A DELIGHTFUL RECENT ADDITION TO THE AREA. THEY SERVE THE FINEST INDIAN CUISINE, PERFECTLY COMBINING THE ANCIENT TRADITIONS AND AUTHENTIC FLAVOURS OF INDIA ALONGSIDE MORE CONTEMPORARY CREATIONS. TRY THEM!

Ingredients

1kg Cubed Shoulder of Lamb (chicken breast, pork loin, or seafood can be substituted)
1 Tbsp Ghee
1 Large Onion (diced)
1 Tbsp Minced/Crushed Garlic
1 Tbsp Fresh Ginger
3 Chopped Tomatoes
500ml Chicken/Beef/Veg Stock
225g Plain Yoghurt
1 Thin-Sliced Green Chilli
1 Red Pepper (thinly-sliced)

Dry Spices

1 Tbsp Turmeric Powder
½ Tsp Cardamom Powder
½ Tsp Ground Cinnamon
½ Tsp Black Peppercorn
4 Cloves
½ Tsp Ground Cumin
½ Tsp Coriander Seeds
½ Tsp Smoked or Sweet Paprika
½ Tsp Chilli Powder (optional)
1 Handful Chopped Coriander
1 Handful Toasted Almonds

Method

Prep

In a large saucepan gently heat the ghee, add the onion and cook, stirring occasionally for 10-15 minutes until golden. Add the ginger, garlic and all of your dry spices. Cook for 1-2 mins to release flavours. Remove the cloves. Add the tomatoes and cook for 5 mins, stirring occasionally or until tomatoes are soft.

Add the stock, yoghurt, chilli and pepper and bring to a simmer. Reduce the heat and cover.

Cook for 1-2 hours or until lamb is tender and sauce thickens.

Add the fresh coriander and season with salt & pepper.

To Plate

Garnish with toasted almonds.

Serve with basmati or pilau rice.

TIP: IF YOU USE SEAFOOD, ADD IT AFTER 1 HOUR AND COOK FOR 5-10 MINS DEPENDING ON TYPE OF SEAFOOD USED. INVITE YOUR NAAN!

Cottage Pie

MOLLY'S CAFÉ SERVES SIMPLE, HOME-COOKED FOOD. HONEST DISHES THAT DO EXACTLY WHAT THEY SAY ON THE TIN. LOVELY BREAKFASTS AND LUNCHES, QUIRKY LITTLE DESSERTS, AND OVERALL GREAT CUISINE. TRY THIS TASTY COTTAGE PIE AND TELL US WE'RE WRONG . . .

Ingredients

500g Lean Irish Minced Beef
3 Garlic Cloves
650g Rooster Potatoes
2 Tbsp Plain Flour
140ml Red Wine
2 Tbsp Tomato Purée
1 Sprig Thyme
1 Large Carrot (diced)
1 Large Onion (diced)
2 Celery Stalks (diced)
1 Cube Beef Stock
125g Garden Peas
1 Lightly-Beaten Egg
1 Handful Grated Parmesan
1 Tbsp Butter
1 Tbsp Olive Oil
Salt & Pepper

Method

Prep

Pre-heat oven to 190°C.

Peel and boil the potatoes.

While cooking your potatoes, in a hot pan, cook the beef mince until brown. Mix in the flour and set aside.

Reduce heat to med/high, sauté the celery, carrot & onion and cook until onions are translucent. Deglaze with red wine, add the beef stock, peas and thyme and heat to simmer until reduced by half.

When reduced, add the minced beef, tomato purée, 3 crushed garlic cloves & thyme. Cook for 15 mins.

Remove the sprig of thyme and spread the above mixture into an ovenproof dish.

Once your potatoes are cooked, strain and place in a large mixing bowl. Add butter, salt and pepper and mash the potatoes until smooth. Fold in the lightly beaten egg and parmesan cheese.

Top the mince with mashed potato and bake for 30-40 mins or until potatoes are golden brown.

Tarte Au Citron Meringue

Created by the vastly experienced pastry chef Robert Bullock, **LE PATISSIER**, celebrates its passion for producing handmade traditional patisserie using locally-procured ingredients perfected by classic cooking techniques and impeccable attention to detail.

Ingredients

Sweet Pastry
90g Unsalted Butter (Irish)
3 Egg Yolks
50g Caster Sugar
180g Plain Flour
Pinch Salt

Lemon Curd
6 Medium Lemons (juice and zest)
300g Caster Sugar
6 Free Range Eggs
150g Unsalted Butter

Italian Meringue
150g Egg White (5 medium eggs)
300g Caster Sugar

Method

Pastry
Add butter and sugar into an electric mixer and combine. Gradually blend in the egg yolks. Next, add flour and salt and mix until dough combines into a ball and butter is completely incorporated. Wrap in film and allow to relax for 30 mins before using.
Pre-heat oven to 175°C.
Roll out pastry on a lightly-floured table and line an 8" flan/pie dish.
Blind bake: Cover with baking parchment and fill with baking beans and bake in the middle of the oven for 15 mins. Remove parchment and beans and further cook for another 5 mins.
Remove from oven and allow to cool.

Lemon Curd
Zest and juice the lemons and pour into a heat-proof bowl. Add sugar and eggs and whisk until incorporated. Place bowl over a pan of gently simmering water and whisk occasionally. Continue to cook until curd thickens, whisking from time to time or until temperature reaches 75°C.
Remove the bowl from the heat and whisk in the butter. Pour lemon curd into baked pastry case and allow to cool/set.

Italian Meringue
In an electric mixing bowl with a whisk attachment, pour in egg whites. Add the caster sugar to a small saucepan and add a little cold water, enough to dissolve the sugar and bring to a boil. Continue to boil until sugar reaches 110°C. You can now turn on the electric mixer and whisk the egg whites until ribbon/lightly fluffy.
When sugar reaches 121°C gently pour over the whisking egg whites and whisk meringue until cool.
Spoon meringue into a piping bag with a nozzle of your choice or just spoon meringue over the lemon curd covering the whole tart.
Gently colour / torch meringue with a blow torch or under a hot grill.

Robert Bullock

I have fond memories of Skerries, having lived in Hoar Rock. I remember gazing across the bay to the lovely restaurants and bars. It was in Hoar Rock that I decided to set up my company and using the local ingredients from the village, began to create a range of tarts, cheesecakes and desserts that I thought would be great for the food service industry in Ireland. Four years on, we are now multi-award-winning (including this tarte au citron) and supply numerous cafés, delis, hotels, large national retailers and corporate hospitality. Employing 12 staff and continuing to grow each year, all from the beginnings in Hoar Rock. Skerries, I dedicate this recipe to you.

A Bit About Wine

In relation to wine and food pairing, don't take it too seriously; no one is going to get too upset if you serve a Sauvignon Blanc with your steak! Also, there is no point in finding the perfect pairing if you don't like the wine.

Here are a couple of simple guidelines:
Match the weight of the food with the weight of the wine. For example, a light seafood dish works well with a crisp, light white such as a Loire Valley Sauvignon or a light red, served cool like a Pinot Noir, whereas a heartier meat dish works better with something more substantial - a young Cabernet Sauvignon in red or an oaked Chardonnay in white.

Another simple method is to look at the provenance of your dish. In wine-producing countries the food and wine have evolved together and are generally made to complement one another. Italian dishes work best with Italian wines!

Now of course there are other factors to think about such as tannins and acidity in the wine. Indeed there is a school of thought that most if not all dishes can be matched with any wine just by "tweaking" the ingredients.
There are many combinations and wines to try. Explore the possibilities and enjoy the challenge . . .

With thanks
DOUGIE STEWART
RED ISLAND WINE, SKERRIES

Extras

Photo – Declan Langton

Coeliac-Friendly Frittata

JANET WELDON HAS LIVED IN SKERRIES FOR 32 YEARS AND HAS WORKED IN CATERING FOR OVER 11. SHE WAS DIAGNOSED COELIAC 7 YEARS AGO AND IS NOW CONSCIOUS OF PEOPLE WITH FOOD INTOLERANCES. A PASSIONATE LOVER OF FOOD, HERE SHE EXPLAINS HER TECHNIQUE FOR PREPARING COELIAC-FRIENDLY FRITTATA.

Ingredients

500/600g Baby Potatoes
(al dente)
1 Leek (sliced)
150g Cooked Chicken (diced)
1 Red Pepper (small diced)
150g Goat's Cheese
8/9 Fresh Eggs
2 Tbsp Fresh Cream
125g Sun-Dried Tomatoes
Chopped Fresh Basil
Rapeseed Oil
Seasonal Green Leaves

Method

Prep

Cook your potatoes ahead of time and let cool. Preheat oven to 180°C. Slice the potatoes in half.

In a hot pan, sear the potatoes in a small amount of oil.

Remove from heat, placing on dry kitchen paper. In the same hot pan sauté the leek until soft, add your diced cooked chicken and cook for 2 mins. Spread this mixture on the bottom of a lightly-oiled fluted pie dish 10/12".

Next, layer your potatoes, diced peppers and sun-dried tomatoes. Top with slices of goat's cheese, 25g per serving.

Beat the eggs and cream together. Pour over the pie dish and bake for 40 mins or until the frittata has risen slightly. Its centre should be firm to the touch.

To Plate

Portion and top with basil. Serve with salsa (see page 118) or sesame slaw (see page 111) and garnish plate with seasonal leaves.

Homemade Guacamole

Terry Roy is a food instagrammer from Skerries - his uncle owned a fishing trawler and parents sold fruit and veg in the town for years. Terry is an avid lover of food and has been on numerous courses including the Dublin Cookery School.

Ingredients

3 Large Organic Hass Avocados
(peeled and pitted)
Juice of 1 Lime
2 Medium Tomatoes
(deseeded and chopped)
2 Tbsp Fresh Coriander (chopped)
1 Red Onion (finely-chopped)
1 Clove Garlic (finely-chopped)
4 Dashes Tabasco Sauce
1 Pinch Smoked Paprika
1 Tsp Ground Cumin
½ Tsp of Sugar
Salt & Ground Black Pepper

Method

Prep

In a mixing bowl, mash the avocado with a fork. Leave it slightly lumpy.

Stir in the lime juice, tomato, coriander, red onion, garlic and paprika.

Next add the tabasco, cumin, salt, pepper and sugar.

Gently mix together and add seasoning to taste.

Transfer to a serving bowl, smooth out the top of the guacamole and lightly drizzle with olive oil to help prevent the avocado from darkening.

Cover with cling film and refrigerate for at least 1 hour.

Terry Roy
I am all about creating and experiencing good food and challenging myself through physical exercise.

Sweet Potato, Black Bean & Cashew Nut Burger

Shoots and Roots is a vegan street food & catering business based in Skerries. Phil trades at some of Dublin's best weekly markets and provides a home delivery service in and around the town. This is health-conscious and plant-focused super food at its best . . .

Ingredients

3 Medium Sweet Potatoes
1 400g Tin Black Beans
30g Cashew Nuts
100g Millet
1 Large White Onion
2 Cloves Garlic
2 Tsp Cumin Seed
2 Tbsp Dijon Mustard
1 Pinch Chilli Flakes
2 Tsp Nutritional Yeast
2 Tsp Dried Oregano
1 Juice and Zest of a Lime
2 Tbsp Rapeseed Oil
Salt to Taste

Method

Prep

Peel, dice and roast the sweet potato with a little oil until soft.

Drain & rinse the tin of black beans.

Lightly toast & coarsely grind the cashew nuts.

Cook the millet in boiling water, 1:2 (1 part millet : 2 parts water).

Bring to a boil and reduce heat to low and cover.

Turn off the heat once all the liquid has been absorbed (10 mins).

Dice and sauté the onion in a little oil.

Mince the garlic and add to the pot. Add cumin seeds and continue to cook until onion is soft.

Add mustard, chilli, nutritional yeast, oregano, lime juice, lime zest and salt.

Combine the onion mixture with the sweet potato, black beans & cashews. Shape into burgers.

Chill and rest for 5 mins.

Fry over a medium heat in a little oil for 5 mins each side.

To Plate

Serve with a topping of hummus & pesto (see page 110).

Additional Info:
Nutritional yeast is a condiment that adds a nutty, creamy and cheesy flavour to foods. It is often used as a cheese substitute and is a rich source of vitamin B.

Phil Smith

Shoots and Roots slowly emerged out of a shift in perception I had regarding the use of animals as food. It began as a personal quest to learn to cook delicious plant-based dishes but has since grown into my own street food and catering business. It's such a joy to cook with a huge range of different flavours, colours and textures. I love my job!

Roasted Red Pepper Hummus

Ingredients

2 Red Peppers
400g Chickpeas
1 Clove Garlic (minced)
4 Tbsp Extra Virgin Olive Oil
2 Tbsp Tahini Paste
1 Tsp Ground Cumin
1 Pinch Salt
Chilli Flakes (optional)

Method

Prep
Pre-heat oven to 200°C.
Cut peppers in half and core them, discarding the seeds.
Roast on a baking tray for 25 mins. Drain and rinse the chickpeas.
Put all the ingredients, along with the roasted peppers, into a blender and blitz until fully combined and smooth.
Add a little water if necessary.

Basil & Cashew Nut Pesto

Ingredients

50g Fresh Basil
100g Cashew Nuts (unsalted)
2 Cloves Garlic (minced)
1 Ttsp Salt
½ Fresh Lemon Juiced
100ml Extra Virgin Olive Oil
100ml Sunflower Oil

Method

Prep
Place all the ingredients into a food processor and blitz until fully combined.
Delicious and oh so simple.

NOTE: THE PESTO WILL LAST UP TO 5-7 DAYS IN THE REFRIGERATOR.

Sesame Slaw

Ingredients

¼ White Cabbage
¼ Savoy Cabbage
¼ Red Cabbage
3 Tbsp Sesame Seed
3 Tbsp Desiccated Cocunut
2 Carrots
70ml Rapeseed Oil
35ml White Wine Vinegar
35ml Apple Juice Concentrate
1 Tsp Salt

Method

Prep

Slice the cabbage using the blade of a food processor or finely slice with a knife.

Toast the sesame seeds and desiccated coconut separately in a frying pan until golden brown. Grate the carrots.

Whisk together the rapeseed oil, vinegar, apple juice and salt.

Pour the dressing over the salad ingredients and mix well.

Spelt & Pinto Bean Salad

Ingredients

200g Spelt Grain
1 Aubergine
1 Broccoli
1 Tin Pinto Beans
1 Red Onion
50ml Olive Oil
25ml Cider Vinegar
25ml Apple Juice Concentrate
20g Dill
1 Tsp Salt
20g Baby Chard Leaves
(mixed leaves)

Method

Prep

In a medium saucepan over a medium heat, cook the spelt grains with a pinch of salt in water. Bring to the boil. Reduce the heat to low, cover and let simmer for 45-60 minutes until the spelt is tender. Drain, transfer to a large bowl and set aside to cool. Dice the aubergine, drizzle with some olive oil and a pinch of salt and roast on a baking tray at 180°C for 30 minutes.

Chop the broccoli into florettes and blanche in boiling water for 1 min. Drain and cool under cold water.

Drain and rinse the pinto beans. Slice the red onion into rounds.

Blend together the olive oil, cider vinegar, apple juice concentrate, dill and salt. Pour over the salad ingredients and mix well.

Wash the shard leaves and add to the salad just before serving.

Jams & Chutneys - Tips & Tricks

Gel Point: 100°C. This magic number can save you plenty of time by removing guesswork. When sugar reaches 100°C - 105°C it has achieved a state of limbo. A state between being neither classed as a solid nor liquid . . . It is a gel!

Adding a few drops of **lemon juice** provides enough pectin to start the process of thickening your jams, helping to avoid using commercial pectin.

A **sugar thermometer** will cost between €15 - €30.

Sterilizing Jars/Lids: Preheat your jam jars in a hot oven for 4-5 mins before jarring. Preheat your lids in boiling water for 4-5 mins before jarring too but be careful, they will be hot!

A thick tea towel on your work area and one in the hand is recommended.

Getting that seal: Jarring goods that have reached 100°C - 105°C will keep for up to 12 months. Getting that seal does not require vacuuming equipment. This vacuumed seal is easily done by using the heat from your ingredients. Just pour the jam/chutneys in the jars and seal tightly with lids. Leave to cool and date.

Leave it: It's very important once you've jarred and sealed, that you leave the jams or chutneys to cool to room temperature before moving to the refrigerator or storage.

The Allotments
Liam Dinneen

This wonderful community of gardeners caters for all culinary tastes and experiences, and developing a richness of recipes, shares its love of sowing, planting, growing & harvesting, producing a plentiful crop of edibles to be enjoyed.

Jams, chutneys, relishes, fruit juices, smoothies, jellies, fruit squashes, dried fruits, poached and preserved fruits, ice creams, vegetable pies, soups, tomato purée, pickled vegetables, vegetarian dishes & curries. The possibilities are endless!

There is work in preparing the soil: the industry of weeding, feeding, composting, enriching & pruning. Finally though, the joy of the harvest: when you pick, eat, share and exchange.

Apple & Pear Chutney

Ingredients

1Kg Apples (peeled & diced)
1Kg Pears (peeled & diced)
1 Tsp Ground Cinnamon
½ Tsp Turmeric
½ Tsp Salt
200g Demerara Sugar
1 Juiced Lemon
100ml Cider Vinegar
1 Large Onion (peeled & diced)
1 Clove Garlic (finely-chopped)
75g Raisins
1 Tsp Fresh Ground Pepper
Dash Olive Oil

Method

Prep

Add the apples, pears, spices, seasoning and brown sugar to a large pot. Add the lemon juice and vinegar and mix well. Cover and leave overnight to macerate.

Day 2

Sauté the onions and garlic in a large saucepan until very soft and slightly browned. Add the macerated fruits.

Slowly bring this pot to a boil and cook on high heat for 2 mins. Turn the heat to low and continue to simmer for 15 mins, stirring regularly. Pour into your jam jars. Label and date.

TIP: THIS CHUTNEY IS DELICIOUS WITH COLD MEATS AND CHEESES. IT IS ALSO A GREAT COMPLEMENT TO YOUR FAVOURITE CURRY DISHES!

🍽 Serves: 8-10 Jars　⏱ Cook/Prep Time: 55 min

Apple & Pear Jam

Ingredients

1Kg Apples (peeled & diced)
1Kg Pears (peeled & diced)
1Kg Jam Sugar, Sure Set

*Selected Spices:
Ginger, Nutmeg, Cinnamon
(all optional)
*Selected Alcohol:
Whiskey, Brandy, Sherry
(all optional)

Method

Prep

Place all ingredients into a large pot.

Add 1 tbsp of your chosen spices and 1 measure (35.5cl) of alcohol. Add to taste.

Slowly bring this pot to a boil and cook on high heat for 2 mins.

Turn the heat to low and continue to simmer for 15 mins, stirring regularly.

Pour into your jam jars. Label and date.

Savoury Butternut & Apple Chutney

HELLA'S KITCHEN - YOU'LL FIND THESE DELICIOUS HOME MADE JAMS AND CHUTNEYS ON SALE IN ALL THE GOOD LOCAL ORGANIC STORES IN SKERRIES AND THE SURROUNDING AREA. HELLA IS A FAVOURITE AT THE SKERRIES MILLS FARMERS' MARKET.

Ingredients

1.5kg Butternut Squash
500g Apples (peeled & diced)
250g Demerara Sugar
250g Onions (peeled & chopped)
2-3 Cloves Garlic
1 Red Pepper
(deseeded & finelychopped)
2 Tbsp Sea Salt
1 Tbsp Curry Powder
1 Tbsp Garam Marsala Powder
1 Pinch of Cardamom Powder
1 Level Tsp Cayenne Pepper
500ml White Wine Vinegar

Method

Prep

Preheat your oven to 180°C.

Quarter your butternut squash and bake until soft.

When cool enough to handle, scrape off the seeds and peel the skin with a potato peeler. Mash with a potato masher and set aside.

In a heavy pot heat onions, garlic, red pepper, salt and spices in a little oil. Add the sugar and chopped apples and cook until soft.

Add the butternut mash and vinegar and bring to the boil. You have to stand over it, stirring, since the mixture can burn.

When your thermometer measures 100°C you can pour the chutney into your strerilised jars.

TIP: THIS CHUTNEY IS DELICIOUS FOR BBQS, IN SANDWICHES, WITH CHEESEBOARDS AND COLD MEATS. IT CAN BE STORED FOR UP TO 12 MONTHS

On Hella

We visited Skerries Mills yesterday and what a nice surprise to find this little gem of a stall. We purchased the Lemon Curd jam along with a trio of Tomato Relish, Raspberry and Rhubarb mixed with Strawberry, Vanilla and Lemon Balm jams. Wow, all are so tasty! The packaging looked inviting and the flavours reflect a real home-cooked product. Thanks, Hella!

Organic Blackberry Jam

Ingredients

1.5kg Organic Blackberries
1kg Organic Cane Sugar
A Drop of Organic Lemon Juice
Special Equipment
Cooking thermometer

Method

Prep
Wash your blackberries and place in a large pot. Heat until boiling and simmer for 5 mins.
Next, add the sugar and lemon juice. Stir until the sugar has dissolved.
Bring back to a boil for 5 mins. Put a teaspoon of the jam on a small plate and refrigerate for 5 mins. Repeat this process until the jam starts to set. Jar it up.

 Serves: 6-8   Cook/Prep Time: 10 min

David Llewellyn's All-Year-Round Vinaigrette

Ingredients

200ml Rapeseed Oil
100ml Llewellyn's Balsamic Cider Vinegar
50ml Llewellyn's Apple Cider Vinegar
2 Tsp Wholegrain Mustard
1 Tsp Ground Black Pepper
1 Tsp Salt

Method

Prep
Put all the ingredients into your vinaigrette bottle.
Shake thoroughly until everything has blended to a nice creamy consistency. Store in the fridge, and shake well each time before use.

TIP: THIS IS A DELICIOUS TANGY VINAIGRETTE WITH A NICE TOUCH OF SWEETNESS FROM THE BALSAMIC VINEGAR. IT IS REALLY SIMPLE, WHOLESOME AND HEALTHY AND IF YOU ARE TRYING TO GET SOME CIDER VINEGAR INTO YOUR DIET THIS IS A DELICIOUS WAY TO DO IT! TRY USING IT WITH ANY TYPE OF SALAD GREENS, HARD-BOILED EGGS, CHICKEN OR HAM.

Fresh Salsa

Ingredients

6 Large Ripe Tomatoes (diced)
2 Cloves Chopped Garlic
1 Handful Chopped Coriander
1 Tbsp Dried Oregano
1 Red Onion (diced small)
60ml Extra Virgin Olive Oil
Juice of 1 Lime
½ Tsp Salt
1 Green Chilli (finely-chopped)

Method

Prep
In a bowl combine all the ingredients. Mix well by hand, cover and refrigerate for 45 mins.

TIP: ROAST THE GARLIC TO MAKE IT SLIGHTLY SWEETER.

Serves: 5-6 Jars Cook/Prep Time: 90 tmin

Organic Tomato & Sweet Chilli Dip

Ingredients

1kg Organic Tomatoes
400g Organic Apples
400g Organic Onions
1 Large Organic Garlic Clove
400ml Organic Cider Vinegar
1 Tsp Sea Salt
1 Organic Red Chilli Pepper
400g Organic Cane Sugar

Method

Prep
Wash and peel the tomatoes, apples, onions & garlic, then dice.
Put the vinegar and salt into a large pot and bring to a boil.
Add the chopped apple, onion, chilli, tomato and garlic. Stir and bring to a boil. Next add the sugar. Reduce the heat and simmer for 1 hour. After 1 hour bring back to the boil, then start jarring. Leave to cool.

Heavenly Heart Pancakes

HEALTHY, FILLING AND FUN! USE COOKIE CUTTERS TO MAKE DIFFERENT SHAPES TOO. PERFECT FOR ANY MEAL – RICH IN PROTEIN, GOOD FATS, VITAMINS AND MINERALS. DON'T DESPAIR IF FUSSY EATERS REFUSE DINNER. PANCAKES INSTEAD!

Ingredients

2 Eggs
75g Jumbo Oats
125g Cottage Cheese
1 Tbsp Coconut oil
Water or Milk

Method

Prep
Blend the eggs, oats and cottage cheese until mixture is smooth.
Add a little water or milk to reach desired consistency.
Melt coconut oil in a non-stick frying pan over a low-to-medium heat.
Coconut oil has a higher burning point than other cooking oils and adds a lovely sweet taste to the pancakes.
Ladle some of the mixture into the frying pan and cook until light brown on both sides.
To Plate
Drizzle a little honey or add a sliced banana or strawberries – Sweet!

Fabulous Fruity Flapjacks

FLAPJACKS – A BRILLIANT ON-THE-RUN BREAKFAST FOR PARENTS. YUMMY SNACKS THAT CONTAIN A PERFECT MIX OF PROTEIN, CARBS, GOOD FATS AND NATURALLY-OCCURING SUGARS . . . THEY'RE REALLY TASTY!

Ingredients

200g Jumbo Oats
50g Ground Almonds
70ml Olive Oil
150g Raisins
1 Tbsp Ground Flaxseeds
or
1 Tbsp Ground Chia Seeds

TIP: YOU CAN FREEZE FLAPJACKS! THEY DEFROST QUICKLY. IDEAL FOR LUNCHBOXES.

Method

Prep
Heat the oven to 180°C.
Put the raisins into a pyrex bowl and just cover them with boiling water to soften for 5 minutes.
Combine the oats, almonds, flaxseeds or chia seeds and olive oil in a large mixing bowl. Blend the softened raisins and water together. Add the raisin mixture to the rest of the ingredients and combine with a wooden spoon. Spread mixture evenly into a square oven dish (approx. 20x20cm). You should not have to grease the oven dish as the olive oil in the mixture should stop it from sticking. Oven bake for 20 minutes or until light brown on top. Leave to cool before cutting into slices or rolling the mixture into little balls.